Autism, Asperger Syndrome and Pervasive Development Disorder

of related interest

An A-Z of Genetic Factors in Autism
A Handbook for Parents and Carers
Kenneth J. Aitken
ISBN 978 1 84310 976 1

Alphabet Kids – From ADD to Zellweger Syndrome
A Guide to Developmental, Neurobiological and Psychological Disorders
for Parents and Professionals
Robbie Woliver
ISBN 978 1 84310 880 1 (HARDBACK)
ISBN 978 1 84905 822 3 (PAPERBACK)

Autism and its Medical Management
A Guide for Parents and Professionals
Michael G. Chez MD
ISBN 978 1 84310 834 4 (HARDBACK)
ISBN 978 1 84905 817 9 (PAPERBACK)

The Complete Guide to Asperger's Syndrome
Tony Attwood
ISBN 978 1 84310 495 7 (HARDBACK)
ISBN 978 1 84310 669 2 (PAPERBACK)

Autism, Asperger Syndrome and Pervasive Development Disorder: An Altered Perspective

BARBARA QUINN AND
ANTHONY MALONE

Jessica Kingsley *Publishers*
London and Philadelphia

First edition published in 2000

This edition published in 2011
by Jessica Kingsley Publishers
116 Pentonville Road
London N1 9JB, UK
and
400 Market Street, Suite 400
Philadelphia, PA 19106, USA

www.jkp.com

Library of Congress Cataloging in Publication Data
Quinn, Barbara (Barbara L.)
Autism, asperger syndrome and pervasive developmental disorder : an altered perspective / Barbara Quinn and Anthony Malone. -- 2nd ed.
p. ; cm.
Rev. ed. of: Pervasive developmental disorder / Barbara Quinn and Anthony Malone. 2000.
Includes bibliographical references and index.
ISBN 978-1-84905-827-8 (alk. paper)
1. Autism spectrum disorders. 2. Child development deviations. I. Malone, Anthony F. II. Title.
[DNLM: 1. Child Development Disorders, Pervasive. WS 350.6]
RC553.A88Q85 2011
616.85'882--dc22
2010030534

British Library Cataloguing in Publication Data
A CIP catalogue record for this book is available from the British Library

ISBN 978 1 84905 827 8

Printed and bound in Great Britain by
MPG Books Group

Acknowledgements

We would like to extend a very special thanks to all the children with autism spectrum disorders and their parents who we have been privileged to know over the years. We would also like to thank the many professionals who shared their expertise with us, and more importantly, share it with children daily. The commitment of parents and professionals alike has become a driving force in our culture. In our original book we spoke of the "flame of hope" that supported children. That flame was fueled by unconditional love and profound hope and has become a fire of positive energy. This energy has led to better diagnostics and earlier identification, new and inventive intervention strategies, and a huge breadth of research across the areas of education and science. We are blessed to be a part of this positive energy!

Personal thanks from Barbara

To my children, Patrick and Jennifer, I offer deep gratitude and blessed love. You have given me my greatest life lessons and provided me great joy. To my parents, Chip and Rose, who planted love in my childhood and continue to bless my life.

Personal thanks from Anthony

To each and every child who has been part of my personal and professional experience, I offer the greatest of thanks for enriching my life.

Contents

Preface

It has been for over a decade now that the broadened diagnostic terminology of the autism spectrum disorders has impacted the field of developmental pediatrics. When we first set out to better define for families the parameters of pervasive developmental disorders in the original edition of this book, the discussion regarding autism had just begun. While the diagnosis had been around for literally centuries, it was not recognized fully as a spectrum of disorders until the later part of the last century. The first edition of this book was intended to offer current and relevant information to educate and support families. The goal of this revised edition remains true to that mission.

We are clinicians in the field of developmental pediatrics. During our active work in the arena over the last several years, we have lived and personally experienced the effects of the expansion of diagnostic terminology in the realm of autism spectrum disorders. We have also been witness to the increased number of children with the disorder. We felt the time had come to readdress the complexity of diagnostic terminology.

The first step following a diagnosis is for parents to have a full understanding of what the developmental disorder means and how their child fits into that diagnostic terminology. Only then can they effectively move on to accept the diagnosis and proceed with implementing the appropriate education and intervention for their child. This book is intended to educate and support families through the difficult process of answering "What does this all mean?" and "Where do we go from here?"

Barbara Quinn
Anthony Malone

Sam Likes Trains

The black and white creature appeared to be sucking his thumb, as the doctor pointed out the small beating heart. For Michelle and Rob this was a moment that they could never have imagined. The first ultrasound of their unborn child moved them to tears. With photos in hand they returned home that day with the security of knowing that their baby was "just fine."

The following months passed quickly and without much difficulty. Michelle gave up her morning coffee and actually counted the pieces of fruit she consumed each day. They explored the many baby departments and finally decided on a Pooh Bear theme for the kindergarten. While carefully aligning the wallpaper border on the center of the wall, Rob dreamed of his child, who would surely have intelligence, athletic prowess, and good looks.

The day arrived. With a combination of panic and excitement they headed for the hospital. Sam came into the world shriveled up, cone-headed, and screaming, but was nothing short of absolutely beautiful to the eyes of his parents. Family came and "cooed" at him, nurses fussed over him and, with the exception of the exhaustion Michelle felt, all was good in the world.

They arrived home within two days and Sam was given a tour of his special room. Stuffed animals adorned the shelves and the balloons painted on the wall appeared almost within reach from the crib. Tucked up in his crib, Sam fell asleep and his parents watched him, as he breathed in and out, in and out. Their baby was home.

Days turned into weeks and weeks into months. Sam rolled over as expected, crawled as expected and climbed onto Dad's lap into his awaiting embrace, as expected. He crawled through the house and discovered intriguing spots, such as Dad's tie rack with the multitude of colors hanging down. By his first birthday, he was walking and giggling and delighted at the sight of his birthday candles.

The following year brought changes for the family. A brother was born, but Michelle felt that Sam had hardly noticed him. The few words that Sam had spoken earlier hadn't been uttered recently. Thinking that this was related to the newcomer, Michelle and Rob vowed to spend more time with Sam, as surely this was all he needed. But their concerns grew. Their affectionate child now seemed content only to sit and play with the wheels of his train. Rob would set up the train on its track and Sam would watch it go around and around, and he would shake his arms and flap his hands with excitement.

The biggest concern that Michelle had, began to reveal itself more and more over time. It was Sam's speech. One Saturday morning during library circle time, Michelle watched from a distance as Sam repeatedly fanned a book with his fingers while the other children attentively watched puppets conclude their story. Eagerly raising their hands, the toddlers shared their impressions. "Mom-mee Babbit!" said one youngster as he pointed at the animated sock. "The Mommy rabbit won't let the baby rabbit run away," shared another little girl. Michelle whispered to Sam, and then repeated his name in a louder voice, but Sam still didn't respond. The group disbanded and Michelle joined Sam on the mat. She put her child on her lap and began to look at a book with him. She tried to engage him in looking at the pictures and urged him to point to the objects on the pages, but Sam was more interested in the motion of fanning the remaining pages.

Later that night, Michelle shared her concerns with Rob. She suggested that perhaps Sam couldn't hear very well. Rob reassured Michelle that "surely all little girls talk sooner than boys" and that Sam "just gets very focused sometimes." He reviewed with her that Sam was indeed talking. He could repeat the end of a sentence and could say some phrases out of his favorite video. Certainly, Sam was smart. He pulled his parents to the refrigerator when he wanted a drink; he was able to run a VCR, figure out the mixing bowl switches, and was fascinated by his trains. But even Rob noticed that Sam didn't consistently respond to his name being called, and he agreed that maybe his hearing did need to be tested.

Michelle was reassured for a while, but other issues kept cropping up renewing her concerns. When friends came to visit, Sam did not seem particularly interested in their arrival and Michelle became exasperated by the amount of supervision Sam needed. She couldn't leave him for a split second in case he became intrigued with the one thing he shouldn't be, like an appliance plug or the hairblower. She discovered that the only safe way to take a shower was to put in a "Barney" tape and he would be certain to stare at that for as long as she allowed the tape to run.

Michelle and Rob found themselves discussing Sam's peculiarities often and arguing about their parenting styles. They eventually agreed that something was a little odd about Sam.

Eric is a Soldier

"Get a load of this!" exclaimed Tim, the proud father of Eric. Tim gingerly placed the masterpiece of puzzle pieces Eric had constructed into its predetermined piece of art. Nonetheless, art to his parents who were amazed at the intricacy and difficulty accomplished by their three-year-old. Many such accomplishments had been shared with family and friends as they delighted in the profound strengths of their child.

In the quiet hours just before sleep, Sally, Eric's mother, rolled to face her husband and once again attempted to discuss the challenges of her day. "I can't turn off Sponge Bob without his pitching a fit!" she shared. "Then he starts going over and over what Bob said." Eric tried to listen but sleep beckoned him and he had heard it before. He knew he could turn the TV to any station with Eric, usually. "Be firm; offer something else that won't bore him. He's just really smart," Tim offered intending to provide support. The light went out and Sally looked to the blank ceiling space hoping for insights to the next day. She knew breakfast would be French toast sliced into equal sized strips, followed by dressing him in his soft sweat pants and Sponge Bob shirt, and heading to his preschool. He would talk to her on the way, reviewing for her their route and always share that Mrs McLaughlin had a mean cat. The cheerful teacher would meet him at the classroom door and after telling her about Mrs McLaughlin's mean cat, again, he would head to the table of cars and construction vehicles. Beside the other children, he would play until his teacher gathered the children for the circle time. He would willingly follow along. Sally would watch the ease of the transition and could leave now, knowing he was happy. Perhaps she just needed to be more structured, or more flexible at home. Perhaps she just needed to be more firm, or easier going at home. Perhaps she...

Eric learned well through his preschool years. Grandparents commented on how smart he was knowing all his letters and numbers. His grandfather offered that he could read words, "He's so smart." Cousins joined at the holidays and Eric eagerly ran to meet them. He shouted at his same-aged cousin to come in as he rallied his peers to his construction vehicle play room. There he talked and talked about his dump trucks and described the given qualities of each.

Sally delighted over the years in the uniqueness of her son. She shared in the pride over his accomplishments. She brushed her challenges with him aside and lived the world according to the rules of Eric. Trips were easy if you took the same routes. Grocery stores were manageable if you offered Eric truck-shaped crackers. And, visits of friends went fine as long as the playmate liked the exclusive world of construction trucks.

Years passed and middle school time approached. The peer world was knocking at the door as a dominating force and Eric had proven to be a good student though often described as quirky. He had some challenges with other children at times, but had been able to be talked through by being offered more clearly defined social rules. Eric liked the rules and did not like it when other kids didn't follow them. Sally started to have concerns that as his peers broke unspoken rules, Eric chose to correct them. It seemed to her that he was going to have a hard time as adolescence loomed.

Eric had moved past Sponge Bob as he became more interested in his construction trucks. Tim and Sally silently embraced the new found interest and then silently watched the trucks become small obsessions. Tucked in back pack pockets and clutched in his hands at times, the small vehicles offered more than play time to Eric. These concerns abated when Eric began reading about the Civil War. He then took on the history world with a vengeance. He was indeed quite bright.

Then came the day the phone rang. Eric, in his enthusiasm for the Civil War had collected various items and memorabilia of the era. He was also quite taken with his own personal uniform. After arriving in school in full regalia, he became the brut of many comments; some from merely inquisitive peers, others from peers driven to be part of the socially in crowd. Eric ran from the building.

"Mrs Allen? This is Mr Phillips, principal of Glen Hill Middle School. Eric is in my office again. I have some concerns..."

Introduction

To the parent/reader

The autism spectrum describes children who present along an expansive continuum of impairments. The diagnostic terminology has expanded and is helpful in more clearly defining children with special needs in areas of communication, socialization, restricted play and inflexible thought patterns. The degree of impairment a child has in any given area, however, greatly influences the individual developmental picture. We are hopeful that this book will further explain how your individual child may or may not fit this diagnostic picture. The reader will see that abbreviations are often used in this field. Autism spectrum disorder (ASD) and the broader term of pervasive developmental disorder (PDD) will be described. Additional abbreviations will be cited as they arise.

This was a hard book to write due to the subject matter, the expanding diagnostic terminology and the desire to serve the individual needs of each child and family. Because children on the autistic spectrum present with such a variable breadth of difficulties, it is hard to perceive these children sharing the same diagnostic term. It is imperative that we look at each child as an individual with a unique developmental presentation. Every child presents as a wonderfully complicated collection of strengths, perhaps with some delays and/or deficits. The child is further individualized by his or her own personality, temperament, and world around them. Taking all these factors into account makes it difficult to understand how we can developmentally classify children at all. However, professionals in this field can be very helpful in accurately assessing these factors and in providing diagnostic information and guidance. Use of developmental diagnosis when a child presents with a particular collection of characteristics is important in helping us direct our intervention and attention. The value of "putting a name" on the struggles that a child faces helps us focus our energies to optimize the child's development.

How to read this book

Some of the information on the following pages will apply to your child, and some will not. Use the information that is meaningful to you. It might be helpful to go to a chapter that particularly looks at your area of concern for your child and read that first. For example, if your main area of concern has been in the language area, you may want to brief Chapter 3 on communication and review the characteristics of language that are apparent in children with ASD. If you feel a need to hear another parent's story before getting into the more technical issues involved in ASD, you may want to begin by reading Chapter 10: Up Close and Personal. This book does not need to be read from the beginning to the end, or in a particular order. Below is a brief overview of the contents of the chapters in this book, to assist you in finding information that is most relevant to you and your child. It is presented to help you best reference and utilize the enclosed information.

Chapter 1: What is Autism Spectrum Disorder?

This chapter is an extensive review of the areas of impairment associated with ASD. It is an attempt to encapsulate and explain the complexity and nature of the disorder. Learning about the basics of the disorder may be a good place to start for some. Likewise, it may be overwhelming and confusing for others. If you find it so, progress to other parts of the book for clarification, and then return to Chapter 1 again at a later time. It is not important to have a complete understanding of the contents of Chapter 1 before moving on. The points addressed are reviewed in detail and clarified in subsequent chapters.

Chapter 2: Social Reciprocity

A descriptive story is offered at the beginning of Chapter 2 that looks at a likely display of the altered social style of children with ASD. The chapter goes on to further explain typical development of social skills and how these skills are altered in the child with ASD. It looks at the wide range of presentations and concludes with addressing some frequently asked questions.

Chapter 3: Communication

The power of communication is addressed in this chapter. Both non-verbal and verbal communication is discussed. Typical development of speech and language is reviewed to set a basis for comparison. Some definitions and differences in communication style seen with ASD are given and frequently asked questions are answered.

Chapter 4: Impairment in Play Style

Descriptive stories relating to play schemes offer insight into the differences seen in the play repertoire of the child with ASD. The spectrum, or range, of impairment is addressed and frequently asked questions are answered.

Chapter 5: More Characteristics and Areas of Uniqueness

In this chapter, additional characteristics associated with ASD are reviewed. These include sensory perception, alterations in motor skills, physical mannerisms, and unusual strengths.

Chapter 6: The Evaluation Process

This chapter walks through the process of having a child's development evaluated. It reviews the professionals who might be involved in such a process and what role is taken by the various specialists.

Chapter 7: What Can Be Done? Medical Perspective

In Chapter 7, an attempt is made to answer the very important question of "What can be done?" The medical approach to interventions and treatments is defined.

Chapter 8: What Can Be Done? Educational Perspective

This chapter continues in the efforts to look at "What can be done?" by specifically addressing educational perspectives and methods. Chapters 7 and 8 are intended to give an overview of options and a preliminary understanding of the multiple methods of intervention strategies currently being employed with children with ASD.

Chapter 9: Additional Options

A brief review of additional options is discussed including discussion on alternative therapies, use of the Internet, and support groups.

Chapter 10: Up Close and Personal

Parents and young people generously share their stories. These personal accounts provide insight into the disorder and offer support. They most certainly communicate that you are not alone in battling with the struggles associated with ASD.

It is our hope that after reading this book, you will have an understanding of some key issues associated with ASD. Additionally, it is our hope that after reading this book you will have a better understanding of your individual child and of how to proceed in promoting his or her development.

Key points

- ASD is a diagnostic way of viewing the developmental style of a child.

- ASD is caused by a physical difference in the brain function of the child. Nobody caused this difference!

- Every child is a unique and special individual.

- The diagnosis does not define the child. The child's developmental presentation and the diagnosis help us understand some underlying struggles.

- Interventions focused on specific areas of impairment can have a profound impact.

- It is a bright future!

What is Autism Spectrum Disorder?

What is typical development?

Before we can have a thorough understanding of what a developmental disorder is, we need to have an understanding of typical, often referred to as "normal", development. Perhaps nothing is more interesting to the human species than the understanding of ourselves and how we grow. Child development has been studied from many viewpoints including the fields of education, medicine, sociology, and psychology. One need only explore the local bookstore to discover the multitude of volumes on the many facets of growth and development. Let's define typical development as healthy development, a progressive changing process that follows along a course of expected growth.

The expectations of progress in healthy development are based on information obtained from observations and studies of a large number of children in a given age range. Appropriate developmental progress and stages are determined by identifying the commonalties among children within an age group. When observing a group of one-year-old children, one is witness to some very inquisitive little human creatures who are very interested in exploring and getting around. Some may be walking independently, while others manage the terrain with the assistance of handy props, such as chairs and coffee tables. The one-year-old curiosity is the stimulating factor that assists in the learning of motor milestones. Furthermore, these little ones may have a few words, or they may not, but be certain that they are able to make their needs known! Whether it is a preference of juice over milk or a desire to go out for a walk, the one-year-old has already established a relatively sophisticated system of communicating with their caregiver. The use of facial expressions, gestures, different crying tones and qualities are all means of communication that are intact in the one-year-old.

It is to be noted that there is a good deal of variation in typical development. Children are not frozen in a moment of time but rather develop over many years, therefore, it is only reasonable that there are variations of the onset of given skills from child to child. One need only look at a kindergarten school classroom of children to see that "Susie" may be speaking in complete sentences while "Johnny" only has a few words. Additionally, personality and individual strengths and weaknesses play into the acquisition of healthy developmental skills.

How does personality affect development?

Let us not forget that children are people after all, and have many things that set them apart from one another. Individuality, our expression of ourselves, is innate to humanity. Our personalities and temperamental qualities certainly influence how we grow and learn. A naturally gregarious infant may smile at the mother walking by, while a more serious baby studies the mother's face for a long period of time before rewarding her with a grin.

Individual aptitudes also need to be factored into the various presentations of healthy development. Aptitudes, or innate abilities, are those skills that come easily to one child, yet may be difficult for another. Janice could take piano lessons and practice diligently for several years, but she may still never become a concert pianist. Kevin, on the other hand, may study piano for the same amount of time, find it easy, and some day find his fingers gracing the ivories at Carnegie Hall! Kevin has an aptitude for music.

Personality and aptitudes may influence the rate in which some skills are mastered, but these individual qualities do not greatly alter the course of development unless these qualities are extreme. Personality and temperamental qualities all contribute to healthy development as long as the personal characteristics are within the range of "normal" and do not overwhelm a child's progress. It is not until they are extreme or out of the typical range that they effect learning, socialization, and overall functioning of life skills.

Mary

Mary, a timid child, entered a birthday party and smiled sheepishly at the sight of the balloons and at her girlfriends. She clung to her mother's leg and hesitated in joining the fun. Once she "warmed up", she quietly joined in the festivities. Though she never became chatty with her friends, she was certainly able to let the hostess know that she wanted chocolate ice cream with her cake.

A shy temperament has not altered Mary's development to the point of severely influencing her understanding of the communication process, or her awareness of what is going on around her. However, being extremely shy, to the point of becoming fearful and being unable to interact at all appropriately, may indeed lead to an altered path of development in the area of speech and language and/or socialization.

Elizabeth

Elizabeth, a very shy child, entered a birthday party and became filled with anxiety and fear. She was unable to release the grasp of her mother's thigh. She could not look around the room or engage in any interaction with the other party-goers. Eventually, the mother made excuses and left the party. The child felt no disappointment, but rather relief.

Demonstrating this extreme of a temperamental characteristic, in this illustration, shyness, may influence the course of that child's social development. Social skills, like all skills, require practice. Play situations, like birthday parties, are the social classroom of the child. If anxiety prevents such interaction, it is reasonable to think that it will alter the path to how a child learns to socialize.

There are many temperamental qualities which flavor a child's development. Emotionality, or how a child wears his or her emotions, varies hugely in healthy development. "Sally" may jubilantly embrace her aunt while "Cody" smiles tentatively at her outstretched arms. To further illustrate this, if Sally greeted complete strangers at the Mall the same way she greeted her aunt, or if Cody ran to hide in the closet every time someone came to the door, one might become concerned about how the child's way of expressing feeling and emotions will impact his or her development. Think of all the personality characteristics of people and the range of presentations; enthusiastic to overly energetic, inquisitive to pensive, cheerful to exuberant, motivated to driven. The list could go on and on. While these characteristics alter the style of a child's development, or flavor the nature of the child, they do not significantly impact developmental progression, unless they are presented to the extreme.

Can personality differences be a good thing?

The answer to this question is, of course, a resounding "Yes!" Differences among people not only add flavor to life, but fulfil the multiple needs of human beings. We need electricians, painters, doctors, and teachers (to name only a few) and there are unlikely to be many people who could fit all of these roles. We certainly need to embrace the individuality of any child and foster the strengths they present to us.

History reveals to us several people who were felt perhaps to have extreme temperamental qualities, which today, and in some cases in their day as well, caused them to be viewed as significantly different. Included among those were some great thinkers and creators. Picasso was criticized for having such a different perspective of the world, but his unique perspective gave us the gift of his beautiful art. Albert Einstein was also ridiculed for his unusual way of looking at the world and his desire not to follow the status quo. He contributed a tremendous amount of knowledge of our world by having an altered perspective. History recounts the lives of several men and women who failed to fit the mold of expected social norms, or who failed to take the accepted vantage point, and yet they left behind gifts that have extended well beyond their lifetimes.

There seems to be today, a heightened awareness of the need to foster the individual strengths of children. It is becoming more acceptable to embrace the differences in children and even more importantly, to facilitate learning and overall school progress by truly accepting that no two people are educationally, socially or creatively equal!

No parent wants to have a child fall out of the domain of the norm. It's a rough road to hoe when behaviors and learning styles are so different that a child needs specialized help and attention. Yet we are reminded by Picasso, Einstein, and others, that perhaps coloring outside of the lines, or looking at something from an unusual angle has great value! How did we come to know that the world was not flat?

What is a developmental delay?

As mentioned, healthy development follows along a predictable path. When a child is obtaining developmental skills along the predicted path but more slowly than expected, they are said to be delayed. For the purpose of illustration, let's look at a car-ride. Our destination is 60 miles (96.5 km) away and we can go between 45 mph and 60 mph (72 kph and 96 kph). That means that our estimated time of arrival is somewhere between 1 and 1 and a half hours. This represents normal development. In the case of delayed development, the car does not change its course, but arrives 2 to 3 hours after the expected time. Let us apply this concept to child development. If a child moved its total body as an infant, but was a little slow to sit independently, and did not walk until close to 16 months of age, one could say that this child is progressing at a slower pace than his peers. This progress is not different. It is just delayed.

What is a developmental disorder?

When we speak of a difference in the pattern or nature of the developmental process, we are speaking of a disorder. Categorizing into groups those behaviors or differences that set some children apart from their peers defines a developmental disorder.

Children with developmental disorders are not merely slow in obtaining skills. What happens in their developmental course is very different not just delayed. Applying this case to the concept above, children with developmental disabilities are not traveling at a slower pace, they are traveling a different route all together. They may arrive at the same point, but they will need some help and guidance along the way. They either have a different way of acquiring appropriate developmental skills than expected, or they have a lessened capacity of acquiring certain skills.

What is autism spectrum disorder and how does pervasive developmental disorder fit in?

Pervasive developmental disorder (PDD) has been the diagnostic terminology for a group of individuals who present with an underlying impairment in the communication process and connectedness to the world around them. This impairment in turn pervades over all areas of development. The inability to fully connect, or relate appropriately to one's surroundings greatly influences learning and the pathway of development. As mentioned previously, a developmental disorder entails a compilation of characteristics that set the group apart from their peers but are in common with each other. The characteristic constellation associated with PDD includes the areas of language and communication, socialization, use of imaginative play and inflexibility in at least some areas of living. The disorder came to be viewed as a spectrum disorder because there is a great deal of variability in the presentation. PDD has been used as an umbrella term that encompasses continuums of impairment in communication, socialization, and play repertoire. This is an evolving concept and usage of terms may be confusing at times. It is helpful to think of

PDD as a framework. Terms used within the framework are autism, Asperger syndrome, PDD (not otherwise specified), Rett syndrome and childhood disintegrative disorder. These all have shared areas of developmental differences with varying degrees of impairment. Additionally, there are unique characteristics to given diagnoses as well.

The evolving face of autism and pervasive developmental disorders

Developmental differences, and the applied diagnoses, are categorized and classified by specialists in the field in the hope of better understanding how children with common issues develop and how best to help them. This is an attempt to standardize, or make consistent the underlying disorder. These classifications are collected in a manual for use by specialists. The manual is entitled *The Diagnostic and Statistical Manual of Mental Disorders*, and it provides guidelines for mental and developmental diagnoses. It is compiled by experts in the given fields and presented by the American Psychiatric Association (APA). This manual is modified and revised over time and maintains a goal of making standard criteria for given diagnoses. This standardization then would mean that a doctor in London, in California, or in New York would see the same child and usually conclude that child had the same diagnosis. Most importantly they could help the family and those working with that child better understand his needs.

Additionally, given the complexities of human development, accurate diagnosing of developmental problems requires significant training. In other words, a person who is inexperienced or untrained could misdiagnose every child in the neighborhood with something when the manual is not used in the context of a significant breadth of knowledge and expertise.

Understanding the manual for classification is helpful in furthering our understanding of the use of diagnostic terms. PDD has been a classification category for a group of diagnoses. As we have come to better understand the unique collection of characteristics and their presentations in individual children, the diagnosis has further evolved and is reflected in the concept of a spectrum of disorder. This spectrum was initially referred to collectively as PDD. Defining a set of characteristics along a continuum allowed for a better grasp of the breadth of presentations of autism. However, a continuum approach became a view of "good, better, worse" or "mild, moderate, severe." This linear model is misleading as the overlapping characteristics offer more complexity than that model allows. Ultimately, the autism spectrum is a multidimentional continuum. With increasing numbers of people impacted by these disorders it has become increasingly more important to clearly define and follow criterion-based diagnosis. For greatest accuracy's sake, a current perspective of autism as a spectrum has emerged as the most relevant perspective.

The core and most critical presenting factor for children with autism spectrum disorder (ASD) is an underlying impairment in social connectedness to the world around them. This impairment in turn pervades over all areas of development. The inability to fully connect, or relate appropriately to one's surroundings greatly influences learning and the pathway of development. As mentioned previously, a developmental disorder entails a compilation of characteristics that set the group apart from their peers but are in common with each other. In the case of ASD, the characteristics include impairments in the areas of language and communication, socialization, inflexible thinking, and use of imaginative play.

To elaborate on this spectrum concept, let us look specifically at the range of impairment in each area. In the area of language and communication, a child's abilities may range from one who is able to verbalize well and communicate ideas and thoughts clearly, to one who has no language at all. Impairment in the social realm can range from being slightly distant and described as aloof, to one who has no direct eye contact or response to their surroundings. Play skills can vary greatly from a child who plays with toys as if they are symbolic of real life, to one who plays mechanically with the movable parts of a favored toy.

It is clear to see how differently any two children on this spectrum of disorders may present. One child may use language to request his food preference at a meal, meet your face to seek assistance, and play rowboat on the log outside. Another may use no words, have only fleeting eye contact and spend playtime spinning the wheels of a toy truck. As illustrated, these two children have significantly different degrees of impairment, however, they are on the same spectrum of disorder. The degrees of impairment in communication, socialization, and play style greatly alter the ultimate course of development.

ASD represents a different pathway of development, which comes from a different pattern of thinking and perspective, than that of a typical child. This altered perspective significantly impacts all of development. Those specific areas of communication, socialization and flexibility in thought are especially affected. In order for the diagnostic terminology to apply, all three areas must be affected to some degree, across a broad spectrum.

The particular components of ASD will be more fully addressed in later chapters. For the purpose of understanding the diagnostic terminology the important thing to keep in mind is that there is a qualitative difference in the development of the process of communication, socialization, and repertoire of play and thought. By looking at these qualitative differences in the development of these children, we are able to look at the individual child and take their own strengths and weaknesses into account. This allows us to set up the most appropriate intervention and educational plan for each child and optimize that individual child's potential.

In addition to impairments in communication, socialization, and play style, often children with ASD have other characteristics as well. These include differences of sensory perceptions, emotional dysregulation, unusual movement patterns, motor coordination and planning, physical mannerisms, and unique strengths. Each child will present with their own nuances, as we all do. When put together collectively they often contribute to the unique presentations of children with ASD. Altered interpretation and perception of sensory input may cause a child to misinterpret, experience, emotionally respond or understand visual, auditory or touch sensations very differently. For this reason they may respond unexpectedly to sensory information. They may demonstrate only minor sensory difficulties or they may be intolerant to certain noises, sources of lights, food textures, or the feel of particular clothing fabrics. Sometimes children with ASD are even fussy about the tags in their shirts or having their sleeves rolled up, or down. A child who does not even flinch when his name is called ten times, may head for the window at the sound of an ambulance siren in the far distance. This "selective hearing" is felt to be in part due to the diminished value of the spoken word and the altered response to sounds. Differences in how sensations are processed and interpreted, and struggles with intolerance of particular stimuli can effect the overall functional level of the child as it potentially creates stumbling blocks to be available to learn both socially and cognitively.

Emotional regulation can be viewed as a child's capacity to regulate their own mood and behavioral reactivity thermostats. Throughout the day, the body and mind is challenged to respond to different levels of arousal within us and around us. The child begins to have self-regulation and self-control and begins to modulate that emotional thermostats. This is demonstrated by their ability to react in a more appropriate emotional and physical way to internal and external situations. Children with ASD often have difficulty controlling that emotional thermostat. This challenge with self-regulation is often made worse for some children by how they are bothered by the altered perspective of sensations. The complexity of this interface is just beginning to be understood.

Unusual movements, or mannerisms, are also associated with this disorder. It is common for the child with ASD to have an unusual gait, hand movements, head movements, or other peculiar body movements. Hand flapping and rocking are often seen and felt to be self-stimulating behaviors. These behaviors somehow cause an internal response in the child that reinforces itself and therefore the child repeats it. These patterned movements may also be a calming technique for the child. While these mannerisms, or stereotypies, are not in and of themselves harmful to the child, they can be very distressing for parents. These movements are visible outward signs of the internal differences in the development of the child.

Children with ASD can also have differences in the way they control their bodies in space, or motor planning. It may appear that the child is not taking in the necessary clues surrounding their environment and moving accordingly. One parent jokingly stated that he thought perhaps his child didn't see the door frame correctly as he had such a clumsy approach to entering a room. Others bump into their own desks or unintentionally hip-check a teacher in the hall.

Another characteristic sometimes seen in children with ASD is the presentation of unusual strengths. Early reading, or hyperlexia, is somewhat common among high functioning children. Some have very good abilities with puzzles, demonstrating skills in spatial relations beyond their age expectation. Exceptional memory skills, such as the ability to recite an entire dialogue from their favorite video, may be exhibited. Children with ASD may also acquire depths of knowledge on given topics well beyond what one would expect for their age. Advanced technical musical skills, or artistic capabilities may be part of this more pleasant side of a baffling disorder.

Additional concerns and diagnosis (secondary diagnosis)

Children with ASD can have secondary medical and/or psychiatric problems that contribute to their difficulties and developmental struggles. One such concurrent diagnosis is attention deficit hyperactive disorder (ADHD). The core concern is that over-activity, impulse control problems and inattentiveness have deleterious effects on learning and functioning. This includes learning and "tuning in" to social skills and communication skills which are at the crux of the problems for the child with ASD.

Obsessive compulsive disorder (OCD) can be seen in conjunction with ASD and is so often a part of the lives of these children that it can actually be one of the determining factors in the diagnosis. OCD is a disorder characterized by repetitive thought and subsequent repetitive actions that are not particularly useful and in most cases obstruct normal learning and functioning. Parents have reported such circumstances as a child having to turn the television on and off exactly 14 times before he is able to leave the room. Another parent reports a child who upon entering his house has to watch the washing machine spin for an extended period of time before he is able to even take his coat off. Some children with ASD struggle with only a few aspects of OCD, while others are more significantly impaired by this condition.

Anxiety disorders may be seen with children with ASD. Anxiety is experienced by all children to some extent but it becomes a disorder when the physical and emotional response is so intense and unpleasant to the child that it impairs his functioning. The apprehension the child feels is not in synch with the stimulus of fear. For example, a child with an anxiety disorder and ASD may be so uncomfortable around the sound of rollerblades on a rink that upon entering just the parking lot of the arena he begins to shout, rock and sweat. Some children may even have anxiety in circumstances that have no precipitant. They may experience severe internal stress for unknown, or undeniable reasons.

Sleep difficulty is yet another secondary manifestation of ASD. Lacking the internal mechanism to calm and comfort themselves, many of these children have difficulty falling asleep, and/or staying asleep through the night.

What is Asperger syndrome?

John goes to kindergarten

It was only the second week of the school year, but the children had begun to settle into their school-day routine. John followed his classmates off the bus and into his classroom without responding to the greetings of his principal and teacher along the way. He dutifully put his things away in his assigned cubicle and proceeded to line up his pencils in a perfect row. This was a ritual he had taken to daily. John covered his ears to the sound of the school bell. His teacher approached him, turned him to face her, and quietly redirected him to the gathering area. He joined the other children on the rug and was interested in what the teacher had in store for them that day. He is an eager learner, particularly if it is an area of special interest to him, like dinosaurs or puzzles. His friend, Jenny, sat down next to him and he noticed the pink ribbon hanging from her pigtail. He began to bat at the ribbon and laughed as it began to swing back and forth. He stroked her ponytail and playfully pulled it. "John pulled my hair!" Jenny yelled as she ran towards the teacher. The teacher reminded John to keep his hands to himself and he looked puzzled as Jenny found another spot in which to sit.

The lesson began with a review of the day of the week, the month of the year, and plans for the school day. The teacher eventually got to John's favorite topic, the weather. Unable to restrain himself from interrupting this time, he began to recite the patterns of Hurricane Hortense. Imitating the inflections of the weather man, John reiterated the hurricane's course, speed of the winds, volume of moisture and amounts of precipitation. Delighting in his depth of knowledge on the topic, his teacher prodded him with questions. "What happened to the land and buildings after the hurricane hit, John?" "How do you think the people felt after they lost their homes?" she asked. John initially looked somewhat baffled by her questions and then returned to his telecast of the 120-mile (193 km) winds.

The fall season progressed and John became more and more acclimatized to the school routines. He followed his peers' lead now and began to copy their mannerisms and reactions in certain situations. He established a friendship with a boy who loved to run a lot and climb in the playground. They enjoyed each other's company and though John could be a little clumsy, he had no fear of climbing and jumping on or off anything. He learned the rules for kick ball and adhered to them rigidly. He got very confused when the other children squabbled over missing the bases or being out. He had difficulty relating to most of the children and began to recognize that.

In the classroom, John revealed himself to be a bright boy with exceptional skills in math and with puzzles. He was also able to read above age expectation, though he did not demonstrate a good understanding of what he had read. His teacher wondered how to meet his needs. In some ways he seemed advanced, yet in others he was immature. His teacher found him gifted in some respects. She also found him a little "odd."

John represents a child with Asperger syndrome. Asperger syndrome (AS) on the spectrum of autism. Hans Asperger, a Viennese physician (the origin of the disorder's name), recognized this disorder in the 1940s, wrote about it and eventually had his name applied to the diagnostic category (see Frith 1991). Interestingly, even though it was discovered quite some time ago, it became only universally recognized as a developmental disorder in the United States in 1994. At that time the criteria for diagnosis were clearly established in the *Diagnostic and Statistical Manual of Mental Disorders*, 4th edition (DSM-IV), a manual used by professionals in the field that outlines standard guidelines for mental and developmental diagnoses (APA 1994).

Professionals continue to debate whether AS is clearly defined as a separate diagnosis from high functioning autism (HFA), a debate that is reflective of the expansion in terminology. When being true to older criteria, AS includes typical onset of language skills and an isolated area of interest. While children with HFA may talk, they may have had a rocky road to get there. Additionally, they may have restricted thinking without having one exclusive thing that they are interested in. This would clinically then not allow the diagnosis of AS by use of older diagnostic thinking. Current thinking would place John on the spectrum of autism with a wide variety of strengths and some areas of deficit. When considering this issue in terms of what it actually means to the child, it becomes apparent that differentiating these diagnoses may not have a lot of practical application. The important point at hand is that the difficulties are in the areas of communication and socialization and those are the areas that need to be specifically addressed. Children with AS, and HFA, who have generally intact language and learning skills, can grow to live independently and have productive lives. It is felt that for most individuals, even those minimally effected, there is always some degree of social dysfunction present. When given the adequate tools as a child, however, in adulthood they are able to use those tools for the necessities of socialization. Daily living requires us to be connected to the people and world around us, to understand the social mores, or social rules of our society, and to be able to interact effectively to get our needs met and desires known.

Language development in children with AS is generally intact and this contributes to the high functional level of these children as compared to children more severely impacted on the autistic spectrum. Slightly more impaired children on the spectrum may be echolalic, or repeat what is said, rather than create their own thoughts and sentences. They may repeat parts of a sentence or reiterate entire passages from a television commercial. As they develop language it may have an unusual prosody, or tone and rhythm quality. Varying intonations and inflections present as a "sing-song" quality of speech. When they are older they have useful speech, but often they remain very concrete in their thinking and communicating. One child with AS asked his mother why the car had bounced after riding over a bump. The mother answered, "There was a depression in the road." The boy responded, "Why is the road sad?"

Social interactions are characterized by one-sided approaches to communication and rather bizarre interactions. Like John illustrates above, children with AS are unable to pick up on non-verbal cues and the subtleties of changes in facial expressions, body language, and other forms of unspoken communication. Due to this, and perhaps because they are sometimes coined as odd by their peers, they have a difficult time making emotional connections to peers and establishing friendships. They may then have fewer opportunities to practice social skills. Tuning in to the child with AS and helping to develop good social skills is very much facilitated by the clear understanding of the disorder and early emphasis on the specific areas of difficulty for the child.

What is autism?

Alex in the sand box

"Want to go outside, Alex?" Mary yelled from the kitchen. After no response, she headed to the family room to check on her son. Alex sat in the rocker swaying back and forth. Mary grabbed the arms of the chair to slow the rocking pace and to try to get her son's attention. Alex began to hum in what had almost become a chant to his parents. It seemed whenever Alex got excited he would make these unusual noises. "Alex, do you want to go outside?" she repeated as she took his angelic face in her hands and tried to look into his eyes. Alex briefly looked at his mom but she did not get the impression that he was actually seeing her. He quickly diverted his gaze and began to flap his hands.

Eventually, after more verbal attempts to get her child to respond to her, Mary physically led her child to the porch door. Though not resisting her efforts, Alex did not show any particular interest in the idea of going outside. Once he saw the screen door, however, he began to squeal and repeatedly moved the door on its hinges until his mother prompted him towards the sandbox. Again, Alex squealed as he began to run the sand through his hands. Despite the presence of toys and tools to play with in the sandbox, Alex ran his hands through the sand watching it spill over his fingers. He seemed to be in his own little world.

Alex represents a child with autism. Alex is presenting as a child with ASD who has significant challenges in his developmental profile. The three characteristics of ASD, namely, communication, social reciprocity, and a restricted view of the world are all significantly affected in children with autism. There must be significant interaction problems and disordered communication for autism to be considered diagnostically.

One need only compare the two given examples of John and Alex to see the great degree of difference in the presentation of children on the spectrum of autism. Though both exhibit deficits in socialization skills, communication skills, and use of imaginative play, their degree of functioning is significantly different. By looking at autism as a spectrum, it allows us to define more clearly each child's individual developmental picture.

The first description of autism was defined by Leo Kanner in 1943 (see Frith 1991, p.93). At that time, he believed the collected characteristics of this group of children to be unique and specific. These children were further defined under the general label of childhood psychosis or childhood schizophrenia. The cause of this disorder at that time was thought to be the refrigerator mom: a mother who was so cold and withdrawn from her infant that she in fact caused her child not to connect fully to the world around them. It didn't take long, however, for professionals to realize that this was simply not the case. After much observation of mothers and their autistic children, it was concluded that perhaps the cause of their developmental differences was something inherent in the child. We have come a long way in our thinking. It is universally recognized that some sort of neurologic dysfunction, or the system of the brain not working just right, is the cause of these disorders.

What is PDD (not otherwise specified (NOS))?

Tom goes shopping

> Tom's mother Sally headed to the grocery store to pick up a few things. She preferred not to bring Tom along due to the trials that arose, but today she had no choice. Seated in the back seat of the car the four-year-old cheerfully played with his bus. "Vroom, vroom," he said as he pushed the bus back and forth on the seat beside his. He took his miniature man and placed him in the seat of his car. "Go to store," he said to the little man. Sally put on Tom's favorite Sesame Street cassette and he sang along as she completed her errand and headed on to the store.
>
> He took her hand as they crossed the parking lot and sat in the shopping cart without resistance. "Tom, Tom," he said while pointing to the soda machines on the way in. "Do you want a soda, Tom?" his mother asked already knowing the answer, as every time they came to the store he got a soda. "Tom, Tom," he repeated adamantly pointing toward the machine. Sally gave him some coins and he deposited them and selected his drink. Tom was able to communicate to his mother what he wanted but had altered communication patterns. He is described as liking to be in the playground but often just runs around the other children.

Tom represents a child on the autism spectrum with what would be also considered PDD (NOS). The core area of challenge for him is social connection. This places him on the spectrum but with perhaps a better skill set in some of the key areas. He is not innately learning how to connect to other children his own age in the playground, but he demonstrates (nice) good attempts at social play with his minature figures. He appears to connect to his mother well but is challenged by ability to communicate. It is easy to see that a lot of children do not fall neatly into diagnostic criteria. When they don't meet fully all three of the core areas of altered socialization, communication and restricted play they are defined as having PDD, NOS. Utilization of this terminology is helpful if and when it helps to direct out energies. When we clearly define the areas of need, we clearly define what needs to be worked on. As a child's development evolves over time, the issues at hand may present differently and this diagnosis may become more or less relevant.

Do we need to label children with ASD?

Parents are very concerned about the labeling of their child, and rightly so. A false label or misdiagnosis may set the child on a course of intervention that is not appropriate for the given child. Also, parents fear the repercussions of the stigma of their child carrying a diagnosis associated with the spectrum of autism. One cannot deny that people have a preconceived notion of what autism is and even today some health professionals and educators are not familiar with the latest in terminology and thinking in this field. This puts the parent in the position of educating the people in their child's world as to what is the particular developmental picture of their child and what would likely be best for them. Let us remember that parents are the experts in their child's learning and play style. The rise in the number of people impacted by the spectrum of autism has led to much greater public awareness and more current understanding of the disorders. Many of the misconceptions related to autism have been put aside. Additionally, many children with many disabilities are fully integrated into classroom settings and are integral parts of their social communities. The face of autism and its spectrum has changed. Professionals in the field of developmental pediatrics continue to help parents and their children by more clearly defining and individualizing areas of concern. The intent then is to direct them onto the right path for the appropriate medical work-up, educational approach, and referral to any other necessary supports.

Looking at autism as a spectrum and specifically defining each child's individual strengths and weaknesses is essential in establishing the right path and intervention for each child.

This label of ASD remains scary, despite better awareness and understanding. The relevance of the label remains in its usefulness in supporting interventions appropriately, and optimizing the growth and development of the individual child.

A recap of diagnoses on the spectrum of autism as they have been classified

- Differentiation of AS; PDD, NOS; autism.

- Key characteristics of AS:
  - ○ Limitation in social interaction expressed by difficulty with peer relationships, non-verbal communication, interaction and interest in others, and expression of emotion.
  - ○ Restricted areas of interest and/or play. Presents as preoccupation or particular focus on subject to the exclusion of broader play schemes or diverse interests.
  - ○ Typical development of language and generally normal intelligence.
  - ○ Can include inflexibility with routines and rituals, physical mannerisms, preoccupations, and unusual strengths (such as early reading).

- Key characteristics of PDD, NOS:
  - ○ Impairment in socialization seen in relationships and interactions with others.
  - ○ Impairment in communication seen as difficulties with non-verbal and verbal language. May have unusual speech patterns and use of words.
  - ○ Restricted repertoire of play and difficulties in applying the social world to their play schemes.
  - ○ May demonstrate some rigidity to change and inflexibility.

    ◦   May present with unusual movements, sensory issues, motor difficulties, and perseverations.

Generally fewer and less serious presentations of these characteristics are seen with PDD and NOS than are seen with autism.

- Key characteristics of autism:

    ◦   Severe impairment in eye contact, social connection and social interaction.

    ◦   Severe impairment in communication skill development inclusive of difficulties with non-verbal and verbal language.

    ◦   Restricted repertoire of play and significant limitation in social play.

    ◦   May have unusual repetitive movements or mannerisms.

    ◦   May not have normal intelligence.

Where does autism spectrum disorder come from?

The differences seen in the development of socialization and language present in children with ASD are based on differences in the developing brain. Conceptualizing ASD as a brain-based condition leads us to look at what is different about the brain in children with ASD. While there may be some physical aspect of the brain organ found with specialized medical testing, the actual neurologic mechanism contributing to the differences in children with ASD is more deep seated in the complex processing that occurs within the brain.

The brain is an incredibly complex computing processor. The most basic mechanism of action starts with a single active brain cell, called a neuron. Neurons send an on or off message to one or many other neurons. Depending on the location and circumstances of those important communicating cells the messages influence movement, thinking and emotions. Some cells call for a specific action, while some stop an action. Neurons must act together. These groupings also work as communicators to other parts of the brain. These intricate cell level communications occur instantaneously and are very efficient in running the many functions that occur in the brain. In ASD, this complex circuitry is not fully organized or as efficiently connected. It is simply not fine-tuned to do its job correctly. This is the basis for the difference in behavior and developmental patterns that are seen in children with ASD, and which show from an early age.

Communication and social understanding are among the most complex of brain functions. When we break down these actions it is easy to see the many levels of complex communication processes that the brain has to accomplish to efficiently process language and social information. The ability to recognize faces requires a capacity to take in the visual information appropriately, process it deep into the brain where it is then applied to a data base of efficiently stored images. The original "photo" is then scanned and applied to pull up the existing "knowledge" of that person. This retrieval is instantaneous and does not take active concentration or thinking per se. It just happens. Now apply to that face an expression of emotion. More complex still, have that face create words. The complexity of the processing just expodentially multiplied. In a child with ASD whose circuitry is not developed correctly, these seemingly simple social reading skills are challenged. Given this new understanding it makes sense that a person's response to their world would be different.

What causes this change in brain development?

While we have come a long way in understanding autism as a neurologic condition, the farther we go in science, the more complex the picture becomes. It is clear that genetic information plays a very large role. Some children with ASD have clearly defined differences in their broad genetic make-up, which result in differences at the more basic gene level. These changes produce a different "blueprint" of the brain which map different circuits. These genetic changes and their effect on brain circuit development, likely lead to the developmental pattern we call ASD.

The genetic picture and its association to the autistic spectrum becomes more complex as we are finding that there are many genes on many different chromosomes that play a role. Genetic research has found that these small internal genes that direct the brain's development are impacted by our outside environment. Environmental influences are vast and we are just scratching the surface of the multitude of potential factors that could be contributing to the picture of autism as we know it today. It is likely that some external factors may play a direct role in altering genes. Others may work in a more subtle fashion as they quietly turn a genetic on/off switch, or alter a circuit by changing the complexity of the brain's connections.

As we continue to investigate the complexities of the brain and the complexities of genetics, we continue to grow in our knowledge of autism. Current trends in research in many arenas lead us to be quite optimistic that a more specific response to "where does it come from?" will be better answered in the not too distant future.

Issue of increasing prevalence of autism

There is strong documentation of the increase in the number of children who are diagnosed with autism. However, it is not clear that there is a true increase in actual number of children or if early and better identification is playing a major role. In previous decades clinicians might have labeled children as having mental retardation, learning disability or as having speech and language difficulties. Some of these same children today have been conceptualized as on the spectrum of autism. It is pretty clear that we have become much more attuned and sophisticated in identifying children at a much earlier age.

Another reason for the increase in numbers of children being identified with ASD has been the change in the diagnostic terminology itself. "Autism" was pretty well used only with children who had "classic" signs: minimal speech and highly disconnected natures. These children unfortunately were not able to have independent functional lives. Previously children may have been thought of as odd, unusual, perhaps with some autistic characteristics but were not considered to have autism as it was defined at the time. Now these children are diagnosed with HFA, autism, AS, or PDD, NOS.

The rate which has soared, however, since the late 1990s now appears to have perhaps stabilized. Of course the concern is that if there has been a dramatic increase in the total number of children with autism, it is critical to discover the reason behind the current rates. Careful consideration of the questions raised are being actively addressed so that efforts can be made to stop the potential epidemic. At this point there are still many unanswered questions, but one thing that has occurred is that there is a significant awareness of the spectrum of autism in our communities where in previous times, it was "flying below the radar".

Social Reciprocity

Social reciprocity is our natural understanding of how we relate to the people in the world around us. It is not clearly understood what brain processes are responsible for this innate connection to our fellow human beings which develops as we grow to a very sophisticated understanding of social nuances and social rules.

"Will you play with me, Jason?"

The cool day did little to deter the preschoolers from playing in the playground on the first day of spring. The "Mother's Day Out" group was gathering for their weekly get-together in which they enjoyed sharing their parenting tales and lamenting on the challenges of parenting. Though not spoken of, they also gathered to assess the behaviors and skills of the other children in the group. The information obtained from such observations proved to be both reassuring and provoking. It was comforting to exchange stories of how to manage "terrible twos" tantrums and to join in laughs regarding failed attempts at "time outs". Yet for Karen, the afternoons shared with the other mothers and their children often left her confused and insecure. Though seldom mentioned by the others, her child, Peter, baffled them all. Peter always enjoyed his time with the group and Karen sometimes wondered why, as he seemed awkward and frustrated while trying to get the attention of the other children. But without fail, before the next time they were to get together, Peter would get excited and talk of his friends.

On this particular spring day, the mothers assumed their positions on the raised bench and sighed with the first gulps of their coffee. Peter had joined the kids running from the car to the playground but as they enthusiastically ventured to their desired play areas, Peter just looked on. Some of the children scurried to the large sandbox and began to shovel and pile and shovel some more. Tommy ran to get his toy truck and hurried back to his place next to Carl, who had already begun to construct an integrated town of curving roads. The two boys exchanged glances and "vrooms" as they maneuvered their cars through the construction site. Jessica and Sarah looked on with little enthusiasm and with questioning facial expressions they communicated to each other their lack of interest in the boys' play scheme. Hand in hand they walked away to the tunnel. They were barely inside the tube when giggles could be heard and soon the tunnel was a pretend McDonald's drive-through. After taking Sarah's order for french fries, Jessica pretended to serve the treat and collect the money. When Melissa came upon the scene she observed the play from a slight distance. It took Melissa a while to warm up in a social setting and, though very interested in joining the other girls, she held back from them. Jessica, always the extrovert, saw her and yelled over. "Wanna play Melissa?" The welcoming brought Melissa in line for a burger and fries. Despite being a shy child, Melissa readily took on her role.

Peter walked by the tunnel and looked on briefly. He stuck his head in the tunnel and was face to face with Sarah, their noses nearly touching. Sarah bolted backwards to achieve some personal space and looked at Peter inquisitively. Peter ran from the tunnel. Other children had chosen to play a game of tag and began running and climbing the various obstacles of the playground maze. As one boy tagged another, Peter looked on. The sandbox caught Peter's attention and he joined Carl and Tommy there. He made no conversation with them as he sat down and for a brief while he was content to move a toy car back and forth in the sand. He looked at Carl and Tommy and wanted badly to be a part of their play. While nudging Tommy, Peter began to recite the layout of the wheels on a 14-wheeler truck "…with vertical suspension and balanced axles…" He again nudged Tommy who had inched away from him. This time it caused Tommy to fall over on his side in the sand. He quickly righted himself and told Peter to stop pushing. Tommy positioned himself closer to Carl and resumed his play ignoring Peter. Peter sat still in the sand. He knew that the other boys were not interested in his story about the truck but he did not understand. They were playing trucks after all.

Squeals of delight, once again, echoed from the tunnel and Peter's attention was diverted to the girls' play. He ran to the tunnel and began to bang on the sides. Loud clashes resonated inside the tunnel sending Jessica and Sarah running out with fear on their faces. When they saw Peter and realized he had been the cause of the loud intrusion, they looked at each other and then at him. "Peter!" They exclaimed in harmony. "Stop it!" They ran off together to the swings. Peter heard Sarah say, "He's always so inflexible" "I just wanted to play," he thought.

Again standing alone, Peter could not decide quite what he wanted to do. He began to play with the pebbles on the ground when some bigger boys went running by. Peter quickly started to chase the older children. They ignored his attempt to be part of their game, but Peter was happy just running after them almost without direction.

This is an example of how a child on the milder end of the spectrum of autism may act in a social setting. Peter's social skills are characterized by a desire to socialize with his peers, attempts to interact with other children and to be a part of their play schemes, and an attempt to share a common interest with another child. These could be considered age-appropriate social skills except that in Peter's case, there is a developmental difference exhibited. Peter's social skills reflect an inability to fully understand the ingredients of appropriate social interaction for his age. He lacks perceptiveness of social nuances. His approaches to other children are often physical in nature, such as pushing Tommy or banging the tunnel, and he does not know how to effectively initiate interaction with other children. He demonstrates a poor understanding of the unspoken rules of body space, in other words, he invades other children's "personal space". Though he initiates conversation, it is not for the purpose of an exchange of ideas but rather more a recitation of factual information. Again, he does not instinctively know how to open a social interaction (for example he may say, "What are you guys doing? Can I play with you?") or continue a conversation (he recites the facts about the truck structure). Peter has an impairment in the area of social reciprocity.

Social development in the first and second year

A young infant begins the process of social development by visually regarding the faces of his caregivers. Young infants demonstrate a preference to look at faces over colorful objects or moving mobiles. This initial establishment of eye contact becomes the basis of social skills. At a very early age, an infant will respond to various facial expressions. Surprisingly, a young baby can show signs of distress when a person looks at them with an angry or hostile expression. Soon the baby is able to elicit facial responses from another. Not only is he capable of reading the expression of another, but he understands that he has the ability to influence another person's facial response. This "reading" of facial expressions continues to progress and at less than one year of age, babies are known to become distressed if their mother or father is crying or upset.

As social development continues, a baby comes to understand that he is a separate, independent, human being. Up until this point, they sense that they are a part of their primary care provider. An 8–11-month-old baby may become distressed when expecting to be separated from the parent, often to the point of screaming and sticking as much as possible to the chest of their mother. Much has been written about this occurrence, which is known as separation anxiety. This can be a difficult issue for child and parent alike. Many a parent has wondered if all this fuss is worth it just to go to the dentist or grab a bag of groceries! However, this fussing is an important step in the understanding of our physical separateness from others, and ultimately in further differentiating this understanding to our social connection to others.

Social development continues to grow with the contact of the parents and loved ones, and by one year of age, a child already has a pretty sophisticated means of socially manipulating his environment. For example, a little girl can bat her eyes and tilt her head in such a way as if to say, "Am I the cutest thing you ever did see?" She in turn knows that this is likely to get Dad to pick her up and play "goo-goo and ga-ga!" A little boy whose Dad had laughed the last time he demonstrated his new found skill of spitting into the bath tub, tries the technique out at the dinner table. He looks to his Dad for the expected response. He is puzzled when his Dad does not find it funny this time, and he shows his confusion with a furrowed brow. These examples illustrate the ability of the one-year-old to read expressions, understand some emotional content to those expressions and attempt to alter the social environment.

With the onset of verbal speech, the one- to two-year-old is establishing another tool to be used in their social repertoire. Non-verbal language, or the use of the face and body to communicate, are also developing during this time. This will be further addressed when we are discussing communication more fully.

Social impairment in autism spectrum disorder

The early stages of social contact, such as the infant establishing eye contact when feeding, may or may not be altered in the child on the spectrum of autism. Some parents report histories of early infancy that are no different than one would expect to hear from the parent of a typically developing child. These parents noted a diminishing of social contact, or a withdrawal from the child's social world. This loss of social progress, or detachment over time, can be indicative of autistic characteristics. With some children, the social impairments are more apparent early on. Parents may report that their child looked at the wall when they were breast fed, or just never seemed interested in being talked to. Some parents report stories of a child who was difficult to comfort or seemed generally fussy. These may be subtle differences and not of particular significance to parents until they are put into the total picture of altered development as the child grows.

Children with autism spectrum disorder (ASD) may not demonstrate typical separation anxiety, as the impairment in social connection is such that to be separated does not necessarily cause them stress. Again, because of the wide range of developmental differences seen in the children with ASD, some children get quite connected to the parent and may have a particular difficulty in leaving them. These children often like routine and are comforted by knowing what to expect of the world around them. Change in that environment may be very distressing. This inability to adapt to new environments, or the strong desire to know what to expect, is often a struggle in the child with ASD. Having and displaying anxiety over separation, or change, in this light is not a stepping stone to normal social development, but rather a representation of the difference in the path of development.

Development of relationships

We have already talked a little about the early relationship to the primary caregiver. The power of this relationship has been well-recognized for many years. As a matter of fact, this is felt to be such an important relationship that often when the child does not develop along the paths of normal development, the mother and/ or father is the person blamed. It was not too long ago that "the refrigerator mother" was supposed to be the cause of autism. It is now universally thought that this is certainly not the case. The early social development of a child with ASD is not about what the parent did but about who the child is! When the naturally occurring process of social development is in its early stages and is not progressing as expected, it is due to some difference in the functioning of the brain itself. It is not fully understood exactly what the specific causative factors are, but by knowing that it is generally an instinctive ability of humans to develop socially, it is clear that this is likely due to something in our programming. And, when that programming goes askew, appropriate social development does not occur.

Peer relationships also start to develop very early on in the life of the child. Early relationships may possibly be siblings and observation of a one-and-a-half-year-old playing with the toes of a new baby sister while cooing in her face, portrays this. Between two and three years children generally like to be with other kids but will play beside them rather than with them. This is called parallel play. Side by side, Allison and Joe play with their building blocks. They non-verbally define individual play zones and proceed to do their own thing. Joe will occasionally check on what Allison is doing and may imitate her constructed tower, or he may even invade her space to get hold of some more red blocks. This will be met with some resistance and soon the mother is on the scene discussing sharing and playing nicely. New skills are learned and Joe goes back to his space, and builds his red tower. Allison then invades his space for some yellow blocks and, although he is initially hesitant to try out the sharing thing, Joe does allow her to take the blocks for her house. The children are very aware of each other, but essentially play on their own. They will interact in the play setting and begin to work on the skill of cooperative play.

Cooperative, or reciprocal play, is when the children actually interact with each other in the play schemes. As they approach three years of age, children are more interested in playing together rather than beside each other. Allison and Joe may still play with building blocks, but as their interaction skills progress they will be seen building a town, with Allison working on the store while Joe builds the school. Soon they are discussing what else they want in their town and Joe helps Allison gather all the red blocks for her house.

Interactive play skills continue to develop and are really very sophisticated by four years of age. By kindergarten children know the social rules required to join a group at the lunch table and what is appropriate behavior to be socially accepted. For example, a five-year-old knows the voice and volume with which to announce his arrival in the library, quietly and politely, versus the voice volume he can use at the ball field, where he can be loud and jubilant. He knows that it would be inappropriate to jump onto another child or sit too closely to a friend at the library table, yet when greeting his friends at the ball field he squeezes onto the bench between two boys. Children continue to practice social techniques and progress with their peers in what is socially appropriate and acceptable. Though social skills are already very advanced in the school age, that is not to say that the process of socialization does not continue to grow throughout our lifetimes. Even in adulthood we practice our social skills. Many of us could cite examples of recent social "faux pas" we ourselves have said or done. Looking at those settings helps us to refine our own social skills. Social training occurs over a lifetime.

Development of relationships in ASD

Connectedness to people around us develops along a predictable and observable path flavored by the child's personality characteristics and temperament. When we say that this process is predictable, that is not to say that children look the same socially. While Amanda has no problem jumping into a circle of friends, Daniel may find it quite intimidating. Both children, however, are socially aware and "normal". Their individual personality characteristics are influencing their social interactions, but not necessarily causing them to be inappropriate. Without this innate connectedness and naturally developing social awareness over time, it is quite difficult for the child with ASD to fit in, or be indistinguishable from his peers in a social setting. Even among the high functioning children on the spectrum, their social interaction is often described as "odd." One parent commented that, "My kid doesn't seem to know how to be a kid." She was referring to her child's awkward attempts at playing with other children, and a sense that, though she could not quite put her finger on it, his behaviors were different and a little bizarre. It is not uncommon for parents to state that their child socializes better with adults. Adults are more willing and able to modulate the interaction to better suit the child with ASD. The nature of the social developmental course is different in children with ASD as they do not pick up on social cues spontaneously or have the ability to apply social skills in a flexible manner. Sean observed a daughter hugging her mother, who was a teacher, in the playground. Later when Sean saw the teacher in the corridor he ran to her and hugged her. Though he had not even met her before, he thought this was how to greet this woman, and he was confused when his classmates chuckled.

The child with ASD establishes a very concrete set of social rules over time and attempts to adhere to these rules in various social situations. This may be, in part, a reason that going to new places is difficult for a lot of these children. They are not comfortable enough with their social skills in unknown environments to know what to expect or what will be expected of them.

Having discussed the nature of the altered path of social development in the child with ASD, now let us acknowledge environmental influence. What we do to influence the child through our interactions in his environment can have a great impact on the ultimate social functioning of the child with ASD. This is particularly true of children with high functioning autism (HFA) and Asperger's Syndrome (AS). If we leave them to their own skills, some will mature and learn skills on their own. However, it does remain likely that they will continue to have problem socializations. Social skills and the rules of our social world can be taught to a good degree, but for children with ASD these rules need to be spelled out more clearly and broken down. In typical parenting we may prepare our children, in that when visiting Aunt Edna, we keep our hands folded and sit quietly on the couch. In this sort of situation we think ahead to let the children know what is expected of them. With children with ASD we need to think about this sort of prepping in all social situations. We cannot take for granted that the children will instinctively know how to act, or will be socially comfortable. This is particularly true if it is an unfamiliar environment where different demands are placed on the child.

By teaching the child what is appropriate socially and providing him with some tools to help him manage socially we may greatly influence the ultimate development of social skill. Looking back at the example of Peter in the playground, he lacked the understanding of personal space and wasn't able to initiate social interaction appropriately. Peter needs to acquire the unspoken rules, and to do so they need to be spoken and taught to him. For example, Peter can be taught not to get so close to other children when he wants their attention, but rather to say something. He can be taught appropriate verbal openers: "Can I play that with you? I'm interested in trucks too!" He needs to have it reinforced not to fixate on stories and factual recitation, as that is very likely to turn off other children. When a child is thought to be "odd" by peers, he is less likely to establish relationships that allow him the chance to practice and progress with social skills. Not only does he then have fewer opportunities to practice, but he may become more anxious about social interactions and decrease his desire and attempts to socialize.

The notion that social skills and understanding of the subtle nuances of a social setting is in part teachable, is evident when one looks at various cultures. For example, it is appropriate in some cultures to bow upon greeting, rather than shake hands. In some cultures it is not socially acceptable for women to show their faces in public, yet in United States culture women showing their faces in public has led to a multi-million dollar make-up industry.

As previously mentioned, the impairment in socialization is across a spectrum. The children at the milder end do not have finely tuned social skills and may be considered distant or odd, while children at the other end are completely disconnected from those around them. The less severely impaired children are more likely to be able to pick up on social rules and the cues that are taught to them.

Temperamental qualities come into play as well. The more outgoing child with ASD may have a stronger interest in acquiring social skills than the shy individual, therefore, the rewards of working on social skills is built into the social interaction. The reward is the positive response from another child or enjoyment of the playtime with other kids. The child who is less interested in working on these skills may need to have another reward system, or means of encouragement, to work on these skills. He may need direct assistance with social cueing and guidance in the social setting until he can establish some comfort level with his own skills.

For the child who is more severely impaired socially, the acquisition of skills needs to be broken down into small components and taught step by step. For example, the first objective is to get the child consistently to look at people in the face. This then needs to progress to components of a social interaction. Conversation openers, verbal responses, appropriate distancing and all the other factors that are looked at when breaking down a social exchange need to be taught, piece by piece. This can be achieved by different techniques and working with qualified professionals who can direct the intervention and promote developmental progress.

Frequently asked questions

- **Why does my child prefer to play alone?**

  This is dependent on the degree of social impairment. For some children this may be because they are not connected enough to others to even be interested in seeking social interactions. For others, it may be that they do not have the social skills to initiate interaction and do not know quite how to go about it. The other thing that may play a role here is how other children have responded to them over time. Perhaps past attempts at socializing have caused other children to shy away from the child with ASD, giving that child fewer opportunities to establish and practice social skills. When self-esteem is bruised the child may come to prefer to play alone.

- **Can a child who likes to be hugged have ASD?**

  It is not true that all children with ASD are resistive to physical contact and comfort. Many children are affectionate while others are less so.

- **Can they have ASD if they had good eye contact as an infant and still look at me?**

  Yes. Some children do not show any symptoms of a pervasive development disorder (PDD) until after their first birthday and up until that time demonstrate completely normal development. Others never had good eye contact and yet others have fleeting eye contact, meaning they will look at you and look away. Some children vary in their eye contact during the day, or day to day. One day they may seem more connected than on another.

- **How can this play out over time? How will they be when they are grown up?**

  This is the million-dollar question for all parents. Let us start by saying that no parent can look at their three- or four-year-old and say they will go to college and marry the person of their dreams. We do not take on the job of parenting with a crystal ball, but in the family of the typically developing child, the parent does not have the fear that their child may not be able to live independently.

The optimum level of social functioning depends on how severely impaired the child is; effectiveness of interventions and social training; acquisition of language and communication skills; and level of intelligence. Most children with AS or a higher functioning presentation of autism have some persistence of social oddity but can live independently and have fulfilling jobs. These jobs are likely to entail skills that tap into their strengths such as space conceptualizing or the physical properties of things. Things that they choose to do tend to have a very specific focus, require concrete information, require repetition and/or are mechanical in nature. They may not demand a great deal of social interaction.

Children who are more severely impaired may have a very difficult time living independently as they do not achieve the necessary social and communicative skills to manage their lives. Managing money, tending to physical and medical needs, and even grocery shopping, are tasks of daily living that require adequate social skills and social judgment.

Cultural awareness and improvement in the nature and numbers of intervening programs should foster long-term hope for families of children with ASD. Many opportunities for community involvement and independent living for all levels of socially functioning adults are being made available.

Communication

A powerful tool

Communication is our means of sharing information, ideas, thoughts, and feelings. The natural evolution of this process is perhaps taken for granted in the typically developing child. We tend to follow closely the development of speech and parents may know the exact number of words a child has at any given moment in time. However, the subtleties of total language and communication development, along with the production of sounds and words, is also progressing over time. This complicated process of communication involves not only the use of verbal language, but the in-depth understanding of the process as a give and take exchange. Non-verbal language is often as communicative as our words. Our body language, stance and positioning, intonation and volume, and facial expressions all contribute to the messages we convey.

Non-verbal communication

Some examples

PAINTING TIME

A group of kindergarten children gathered around the craft center. Mary takes her spot as far from Judd as she can. She recalls the last time she painted with Judd when he splattered red dots all over her creation. Her eyes meet his and she holds his gaze. "I remember what you did, Judd!" she communicates with her stare. She steps a bit farther down the table letting him know for sure that she "was going to keep her distance." Judd's facial expression softens as he drops his head slightly. He briefly lifts just his eyes as if to say, "I'm sorry. I didn't mean to do it." Mary does not take his non-verbal apology well and busies herself setting up her supplies. "I don't forgive you. Keep your distance!" she communicates clearly, without saying so much as one word.

This example illustrates how integrated communication is even before the school years. We perfect these techniques as we grow and establish powerful extensive non-verbal skills for use throughout our lives.

A BOARD MEETING

A group of people were sitting around a conference table. One shares an idea and then to reassure himself of the others' approval adds, "You know what I mean?" He does not really intend to ask if the others understood the sentence he just spoke, he is asking for reassurance. He leans forward resting his arms on the table, and looks to get eye contact with one of the other parties present, further communicating, "Would someone please agree with me?" The first person he connects with eye to eye, diverts her gaze and fiddles with the stirrer in her cup of coffee communicating, "Don't want to touch that with a ten foot pole!" At the end of the table, a gentleman busies himself jotting on a piece of paper, communicating, "I'm busy with something else right now, can't address your question." One person at the table is caught in his gaze and he slightly nods, indicating, "Come on, say something!" and the person responds with arms folded while leaning backwards in his chair. "I see what you're saying." His words hedge true agreement and his body language clearly confirms, "I don't really agree with you!"

This very basic example of a communicative exchange demonstrates how much we communicate to each other daily with, and without, our words. Communication is a very sophisticated process and a very powerful tool in the functioning of the human being.

Children with autism spectrum disorder (ASD) have an underlying impairment in the process of communication. An inability to use speech and language as an effective means of communicating as well as a lack of understanding the natural course of conversing, or the give and take exchange, pervades over the total developmental style and functioning of the child.

Communication early on

Typically, developing children understand the power of communicative exchange as a tool very early on. Young infants recognize that different cries are used to communicate different things. Sitting outside the door of a six-month-old's bedroom, one first hears some arousal from her nap. A few gurgle sounds and raspberries are heard. Shortly after she begins her whiney soft cry indicating, "I'm awake now. Someone come get me!" The whine becomes louder communicating, "Do you hear me?" The volume and tone are harsher, "Hello, anybody home?" Until at last a full-blown wail ensues, "I want out of here, NOW!" A child naturally comes to understand that she can manipulate her world by this wonderful game people play back and forth, called communication.

Following the establishment of early eye contact, facial expressiveness, vocalizations and early sounds, whining and crying, comes the progression of gesturing. By six months children will wave "bye" and raise their arms when they want "up". They even start pointing for requests and/or choices. These early non-verbal means of getting their needs met sets the stage for later speech and language development. Early connection and this natural progress of conversing are the milestones that set a solid base for the entire communication process.

By one year of age, many children have a few words, with a word defined as a sound that consistently means the same thing. The sound "ba" can be a word if it is consistently used to mean "bottle". By two to three years of age, children are putting words together and beginning to make short sentences. They share thoughts, wants, and concerns with their words, and their non-verbal skills. A toddler eagerly tells his mom that he saw a rabbit in the back yard. Even if his only true words are "babbit" and "out", he is able to share his story with enthusiastic intonation, excited facial expressions, and gestures for his entire story. And, most importantly, he is interested in sharing his experience.

There is a great deal of variation among typically developing children in the area of speech and language. This is mostly, however, in the area of expressive language, or the use of words. Some one-year-olds have as many as ten words, while some one-and-a-half-year-olds are just starting to say some words consistently. Both of these sets of children may be considered to have normal speech if they are understanding language, communicating without words appropriately, and are interested in sharing wants, needs, likes and dislikes, and experiences with the people in their world.

Breaking the code

The process of learning language includes learning the code, or grasping the symbolism of words. This also entails being able to use language in and out of context. The code includes the letters, their sounds, and syntax and grammar. The rules of this code start to be learned by an infant and are nearly fully understood by five to six years of age. The understanding of symbols includes initially assigning meaning to concrete words, such as "table", and progresses to actions, such as "running". Eventually these symbols are assigned to concepts, such as "love". While vocabulary is constantly being expanded upon and changed, even in adulthood, a vocabulary of several thousand words is already present in the preschooler.

The meaning of language in and out of context is the most sophisticated piece of learning in the language system. This includes understanding the meaning of a phrase by applying social and circumstantial information. To illustrate this point let's look at the words "hot dog." There is a difference between a hot dog, a frankfurter in a roll; a "hot dog," a kid doing flashy tricks on his skateboard; and a hot dog, a warm canine. One must apply more advanced understanding of the context the word is used in to accurately assign its meaning. Humor, irony, sarcasm, figurative speech, poetry, and other advanced uses of the human language, all rely heavily on the listener's ability to understand in context and to broaden their understanding to a brand new context.

A recap

With appropriate connectedness, children learn early on that communication is a powerful means of having their needs met. This is accomplished by non-verbal and verbal means. The communication process advances to the production of gestures and then words. In its more advanced stages, language in linked to symbolism and imagination. The code is then more fully understood and we are able to advance to the point of de-contextualization, or the ability to apply various meanings to the same words, based on the context it is used in. As you can see, communication is quite a sophisticated process, which we often take for granted in the typically developing child.

The spectrum of impairment in communication seen with ASD is not only in language development, but is seen in the entire communication process. While some minimally affected children are relatively good communicators, others are more severely impaired in this area. There is always some degree of communication impairment in all children with ASD. The degree of severity of the impairment greatly influences the overall developmental growth and optimal functioning of the child.

Asperger syndrome (AS) is characterized in part by superficially typical speech development. This "normal" speech pattern, however, is frequently atypical. The communication patterns seen in AS have an altered quality. The fact that these children may have fairly good speech does contribute often to their high level of functioning. Though they have words and can use words effectively, they are usually very concrete in their thinking and communicating. They often have difficulties with the use and interpretation of non-verbal cues. They are likely to have long-standing difficulties with the subtleties of communicating and understanding the emotional components of a communicative exchange. Children with AS and those on the high functioning end of the spectrum are often awkward in their attempts to initiate and maintain a normal conversation.

The autism spectrum disorders are characterized by a wide variation of communicative functional levels. It is a fallacy that all children with ASD are non-communicative or that they do not want or desire to communicate effectively with their peers. Though this area is always affected to some degree, the presentation of the disorder changes greatly depending on the ultimate level of functioning in this area. Obviously, if a child has language and has a desire to relate to his peers to some extent, he will be more able to develop social and communication skills than the child who has little to no language and a lack of desire to socialize, or connect, to another child.

It is not uncommon for parents of AS and ASD children to have concerns about their child's hearing, because the child doesn't consistently respond to being called. It is usually not the hearing that is the cause of this lack of response, however; it is more due to the focus of their listening. Children with ASD may not even turn when their mother calls their name 17 times with various volumes and intonations. They will, however, cover their ears when the phone rings. They have what might be considered very selective hearing, or more accurately, very selective listening.

The child with AS and other high functioning children with ASD may have good language skills but seem odd in their conversing, in that they are more likely to have committed learned words and phrases to memory. They have difficulty applying necessary flexibility and appropriate social rules to a given setting, or to a conversation. When their social skills and communication skills are challenged in a conversation with a typically developing child, the child with ASD may revert to sharing information that is rote and more comfortable to them. For example, they may appear to be reciting information about an area of interest, or repeat a favorite jingle, rather than appropriately respond to another child's question.

Compounding the problem of learning good communication skills is the fact that often children with ASD are viewed as odd by their peers so they are given less of an opportunity to practice communication and social skills. Children with ASD can be aware of the struggles they have and certainly can be aware that other children do not want to be with them sometimes. This makes them more uncertain of themselves and less likely to want to challenge and expand their skills. As for people who go to foreign places, they learn the language ahead of time only to discover that the culturally specific use of language changes the foreigner's ability to interpret or to carry on a conversation. For the child with ASD, perhaps it is as if he is a foreigner in his own land.

Children with autism, and the more severely impaired on the spectrum of autism, have more severely impaired speech and language development. Some have no words, others have words but cannot use them appropriately. In these children, the impairment in the socialization process and the communication process are both so hindered that independent functioning in later years is unlikely.

As stated, children between the mild end of the autistic spectrum to those more severely impaired have many different presentations and qualities to their speech and communication techniques. The terminology for the type of communication disorder that children with ASD have is referred to as a semantic pragmatic communication disorder. The disorder is characterized by inaccuracies of semantics (or the structuring of words into meaningful phrases), and poor pragmatics (or the social aspect of the communication process).

Some definitions

Semantic disorder: The inaccurate structuring of words into meaningful phrases.

Pragmatic disorder: Lack of connection in the communication process. Inability to grasp the social component of conversing.

The core deficit in communication struggles for children with ASD centers around semantics and pragmatics. How to put words together to make sense and how to connect that to the social circumstances they are in is exceedingly difficult for these children.

Echolalia: The repeating of part or all of a sentence. Described as "ping pong" language, the same words go back and forth, but nothing meaningful is exchanged.

"Johnny, do you want an apple?" "Wan an apple." "You want an apple?" "Wan an apple." When given the apple he puts it on the table. He was just repeating the words, not making a request.

Pronoun reversal: The inaccurate usage of pronouns.

"He likes meat balls." The child meant, "I like meat balls." "Give it to him," instead of "Give it to me."

Reversal of meaning: What they say is not what they mean.

A child with AS is on the phone to his mother. "Is mother here?"

Recitation: Repetition of something that they heard.

"It's the real thing. Coke is. That's the way it should be!" Used in conversation and not intended to communicate anything in particular.

Associations and recitation: These are used rather than appropriate words.

A child seeking milk in her cereal always says, "Does a body good!" She is attempting to communicate something in particular but is using the wrong words.

A child who is familiar with computers says, "Click here" at every stop sign on the road. (That is an icon often used to exit children's programs.) He is attempting to communicate that he wants to get out of the car.

Factual: Recitations rather than conversation.

When asked about what he did last night, a child recites the weather forecast, verbatim.

"Winds were out of the east at 40 miles per hour…" His vocalizations mimic that of the weather man.

Concrete thinking: Evident in their language.

After riding over a large bump the mother explains that there was a "depression in the road," the child with ASD asks, "Why was the road sad?"

Use of language out of context: The inappropriate changing of topic or flow of conversation.

A child in a conversation about sandcastles begins to talk randomly about Beluga the whale.

Inability to make appropriate openers: Not being able to initiate a conversation.

A child trying to play with other children runs up to them spontaneously and says, "Party of four, your table is ready!"

Unusual prosody: The pitch and cadence of speech.

Also, described as a "sing song" nature to their speech pattern. They may sound like they are singing or speaking another language.

Unusual tone or volume: Vocal quality is different without physiological cause. They may sound monotone.

Frequently asked questions

- **Why was my child slow to talk and then came out with full phrases?**
  Language development is not delayed but different in these children. The reason this pattern occurs is not clearly understood. Language is such a social act that problems in relating and difficulties with socialization are almost always coupled with impairments in the communication development of children with ASD.

- **Why does my child echo me?**
  Echolalia is commonly seen and it is a part of the confusing picture of language development in children with ASD. Because they don't grasp the give and take process of communication, they are more likely to copy, or recite, than add onto an idea or expand on a thought.

- **How is it that my child can recite an entire video and not say he wants juice instead of milk?**
He does not understand the power of communication as a tool to meet his needs and wants. Children with ASD frequently do well with the rote aspects of language. They are good imitators and have highly developed memories, but only for some things.

- **Why does my child pull me everywhere?**
This is a more primitive way of getting some needs met. Usually children will do this for basic needs. If gestures and words are missing, then a physical prompt may be the only way for the child to communicate.

- **Does my child have normal hearing?**
Generally, children with ASD have good hearing but lack good listening skills. They may be selective in what auditory stimuli they respond to. A child may not seem to notice you closing a door behind them, but the same child covers his ears when the blender is turned on. While hearing loss is not typically associated with ASD, if adequate hearing is questioned then testing is indicated.

- **How will this play out over time?**
Children with ASD, particularly those on the milder end of the spectrum, may develop good language skills. It is likely, however, that most will persist to have some degree of difficulty in understanding the subtleties of the human language and its abstract meanings. They will likely remain concrete in their thinking and conversing.

A final note

Language skills are crucial to the overall, optimum development of a child with ASD. It is critical to address this issue promptly and vigorously.

Impairment in Play Style

The playroom is the classroom for the young child. It is in this classroom that we can learn a great deal about how a child is learning and developing. The way in which a child manipulates toys, explores his environment, sets up play schemes, and interacts with others in play, tell us not only how a child is learning, but also how he is assimilating and relating information from the world around him. It is in the playroom that children with pervasive developmental disorder (PDD) reveal yet another difference in their style of development.

Chelsea

Locks of red curls bounce as Chelsea, a three-year-old, enters the play corner of the doctor's office. A kitchen set catches her interest as she checks out its cabinets and shelves. Finding some miniature pots, Chelsea sets about the task of making pretend soup. Small blocks are stirred in a pan as she asks her mother if she would like some soup as well. She pretends to wipe her hands on her apron as she's certain this is what one does when the soup is ready to be served. She has observed her mother do this many times. No soup bowls are to be found, so Chelsea makes do with a teacup and carefully pours the imaginary food into the cup. Carefully, balancing it to avoid any spills, Chelsea carries the tray to serve her mother, who tastes the invisible soup and compliments the chef. "Would you like some crackers with that?" she asks her mother.

Randy

Randy holds tight to the grasp of his mother's hand as he enters the doctor's office. Not one of his favorite places, Randy hovers behind his mother's leg as she signs them in. While waiting, Randy spots the knobs on the play kitchen set up in the corner. As he pulls his mother with him, he approaches the play area. Baskets of colorful building blocks, dolls, and other toys surround the inviting children's corner. Randy's mother picks out a dump truck and tries to engage Randy. "Oh Randy, look what I found?" she entices. Randy seeks his own toy as he rummages through the large bucket. As Randy's mother returns to her seat, he begins to line up an assortment of Matchbox cars. He continues to add one after the other to form long rows. The rug directly under him is decorated with streets and a town designed to use with cars, but Randy does not seem to notice, or show any interest in the cars driving through the pretend town. He remains content to align his cars.

The difference in these two children's play certainly illustrates the potential difference seen between the play style of a typically developing child and one with autism spectrum disorder (ASD). These examples are given for the purpose of clarifying the difference but it must be noted that the difference can be much more subtle. Again, each child has an individual presentation and may have a greater or lesser degree of impairment in this area.

Let us look more closely at these two examples to explain more fully the issue of a child's play repertoire, or a child's inclusion of skills and social understanding in their play. Chelsea recognized the connection of the pretend kitchen set to a real kitchen. She was able to apply her understanding and observations of her mother's role in the kitchen into her imaginary play scheme. This application of real life events into a child's play is a way for the child to practice what goes on in the real world around them. It affords them the opportunity to imitate appropriate social behavior and learn from the imitation of others' behaviors.

The ability to make a connection between the pretend and the authentic is observed early in a child's life. Young children will imitate combing hair, feeding a doll, or hugging a stuffed animal. They indeed have the capacity to apply the use of imagination to set up a pretend world that mimics a real social world around them.

Now let us look at Randy's selected play. First, the hesitation to step into new play environments is apparent for some children with ASD. Often the need to know what to expect or anticipate from a given situation may preclude them from becoming interested in toys in such an environment as the doctor's office. The knobs of the kitchen set were the first enticing item. Randy then proceeds to mechanically investigate the Matchbox cars. He spins the wheels and manipulates them for the purpose of examining their parts, but misses what they are, as a whole, an imitation of a real life automobile. He does not attempt to apply the cars to the rug-town streets, or demonstrate an understanding that these miniatures represent, or symbolize, something in his world. Randy misses any broader play scheme, while he physically explores, rather than applies an imagination to his repertoire. The lining up of items also is something commonly seen when watching a child with ASD play. Sequence and order seem to, in some way, give pleasure and are a predominant theme of much play for many of these children.

Spectrum of impairment

A child with Asperger syndrome (AS) and those mildly affected on the spectrum of ASD may have very minimal impairment in this area. They may have the capacity to find the symbolism of toys and can apply that understanding to their play. They may demonstrate the use of imagination to apply their understanding of their real world to their pretend play. Often, their difference in social understanding can be revealed in play. While a typically developing child imitating his father mowing the lawn may interject visiting with a neighbor, the child with ASD fails to see any relevance to the exchange and is more interested in the mowing action. A child with ASD may not choose play schemes that are socially loaded to begin with as this just doesn't catch their fancy. Playing school, for example, with a group of dolls may not be desirable to a child with ASD. While they may play school, they may not apply a lot of social interacting and relating with the dolls. The child who can use a log as a rowboat, has to have a real oar, and no one is asked to join him in his boat.

As you can see in the higher functioning children with ASD, the impairment in play repertoire, or use of imagination in their play may be very subtle. As one moves along the spectrum, however, the impairment becomes more noticeable. Children more severely impaired may spend a great deal of time lining things up in rows. They may be content to spend a good deal of time moving one given part of a toy rather than applying it to any imaginative play. Play is observed to be very repetitive and in some cases to the point of restricting them from moving on to other toys or activities. In addition to this repetitive pattern of play, the child with ASD may have a repetitive pattern to what they choose to play with. Parents often report that their child is particularly taken with one toy, or category of toy. For example, trains have an incredible appeal to many of these children and we can only guess that this is related to the fact that they run in sequences. It is not uncommon for the child with ASD to be so interested in one area or topic, that they develop quite a particular knowledge in that area. For example, a child may know and be able to identify all the characters for the "Thomas the Tank Engine" series, or know all the names of dinosaurs. This limited degree of interest is a prominent characteristic of the disorder. A depth of knowledge is not necessarily a bad thing, but a problem arises when it is to the exclusion of other play, or restricts participation in more socially loaded interactions.

With a greater degree of impairment and an even more limited repertoire of play, the child with ASD may be more physically driven. Play may be observed to be internally driven and of a physical nature; running around in circles and not seeming to notice play apparatus or toys, repetitively throwing toys over the back of the couch, and content to do this over and over again, or to be content to look up at a fan and hum. These all represent the most severely impaired along the spectrum. Their lack of connection to the world around them influences their development to the point where there is no appropriate play to represent a social world.

Certainly, the issue of whether a child will be able to play effectively with trucks when he is 20 years old is not the point. It is the greater picture of the basic understanding of the social symbolism in things, and that the world is not a concrete setting but rather changes with varying social settings and varying environments. Think back to the illustration of Eric is a Soldier at the beginning of our text. It looked at this concept of inflexibility in the application of social rules and subtle connections. These are the skills gained after accomplishing the classroom of childhood; the playroom.

Play may also demonstrate that a child with ASD may have differences in their expression of sensations and feelings. Strong likes and dislikes for different sensory experiences are readily apparent when a child simply cringes to touch sand while able to pour water over a tower repeatedly. For another child with ASD, the reverse may be true. The processing of sensations has a wide breadth of presentation and is not exclusive to tactile input. Perception of visual, auditory, temperature and movement awareness all offer additional components to the individual play presentations of children with ASD.

Frequently asked questions

- **How does this play out over time?**
  The optimal functioning of any child with ASD very much depends on all areas of impairment, and they do all inter-relate. A child with a more severe social impairment may not work on communication skills to the extent of a child who is more socially adept. In turn, a child with more limited social skills is less likely to apply those to their play schemes, or expand on social learning through play.

- **Why does my child always line things up in rows?**
  Sequencing and repetition are certainly a theme of play for many of these children. A sense of order seems to be comforting to them. And again, they may not see or be

interested in the symbolism of toys. Predictability is also a need illustrated in patterned play.

- **Why does my child always play with the same things?**
  Children with ASD do seem to stick to the same items over time. Some certainly expand on that theme, but many choose one item to the exclusion of a whole world. It is their comfort with sameness and discomfort with change that probably contributes to this.

- **Why does my child become fascinated with just one aspect of the toy?**
  Physical manipulation of a toy is common among children with ASD. They focus on the movements of a toy, or the mechanical parts. They miss the bigger picture, so to speak. There may also be a visual or sensory component contributing to their choice of toys. A child may enjoy watching the reflection of light created by opening and closing a play house door rather than being intrigued by the play figures that could be entering the house to join in a pretend snack time.

More Characteristics and Areas of Uniqueness

Alteration in sensory perception

We are fortunate today to have adults who were diagnosed with autism as children and now are able to share their perception of sensory input. Because we cannot get inside the head of a child with autism spectrum disorder (ASD) to hear as they hear, feel as they feel, see what they see, this shared information has confirmed that children with this disorder have a different way of filtering sensory input and making sense of it. It is for this reason that some children will be particularly sensitive to sounds, lights, touch and the sensations of balance or equilibrium. The same child who won't so much as look up when you ask if he wants more milk, three times at the dinner table, is the child who hears the fire siren four blocks away, or covers his ears when the radio is turned on. Perhaps, for one child the flashing on a computer game is just too irritating, while for another it is fascinating to watch the flashing lights. The alteration in sensory processing may cause one child to insist upon wearing long pants in the heat of winter and yet another child is not even able to tolerate the tags inside the back of his shirt collar. The inability to tolerate some touches is called tactile defensiveness. This can even carry over to textures of food that a child will not eat. The sensitivity to food textures can be so aversive to a child that food intake can be very restricted. Furthermore, the alteration in the processing of sensations may impact the physical movements of a child with ASD. It is largely felt that some of the tendency toward being clumsy or looking awkward in certain movements is not the result of a difference in the motor system itself. It is rather due to the child's altered perceptions of surrounding space and awareness of their body movements.

There is a great deal of variation from child to child with regard to what sensory stimulation is enjoyed, as well as what is intolerable. This altered process dramatically influences a child's reactions to the outside, stimulating world. As adults, we take for granted the ability to filter sensory information. When sitting across from a friend at the lunch table we are able to focus on the conversation. We will not be tremendously distracted by the noises of others in the cafeteria, or the slight flickering of the fluorescent lights overhead. Think of how difficult it would be to connect socially to our friend across the table from us if all the sensory input around us received equal processing value. Imagine that the clanking of the dishes in the removed kitchen, the laughter of a woman, the whimpering of a child, and the annoyance of the surface of the wrought iron chair were compiled at the restaurant table offering a cacophony of sensations. Then the food arrives with an unfamiliar aroma on top of all that. It would be exceedingly difficult to carry on a conversation, let alone eat, in such an over-loading environment. It is felt that many children with ASD struggle with the challenge of processing and filtering just such information. This in turn negatively impacts a child's ability and desire to socially interface when multiple forms of sensory information cloud their altered social screening.

How do we perceive?

This question has been the subject of scientific and philosophical debate for years. Much more complex than simply the reception of information through eyes, ears, or skin, it is also the interpretation of that information that comes into play. Memory, emotion, combinations of sensations are all involved. We can only begin to have a shared understanding of perception because we probably have similar ways of sensing our world. The antithesis is also true, however. It is clear that everyone does not have similar ways of interpreting sensations and understanding the world. Did Mozart hear music like others? Did Monet capture and interpret light like others? Does Tiger Woods perceive the distance from his hand to the green like others?

While we can't fully understand just how others perceive, we can be certain that there is variability among the general population. Mozart may have seen music in his mind's eye, visually composing as if painting a picture. Perhaps this gave him an ability to conceptualize the total composition rather than the individual details. How did Einstein perceive and understand math? He had a capacity for looking beyond numbers to see the more expansive patterns of numbers. He did not merely look beyond what others had studied; he studied things differently. These examples help us to understand that, while most of us probably have a degree of shared perceptions, there is variability in those perceptions, and some people view the world in a very different light. While physical input may be the same, the intellectual perception, or interpretation, is different. It is very possible that this is the core difference in sensory processing for many individuals with ASD.

Without a means of filtering out stimuli, or weeding out the sights and sounds that are not useful at a given time, a child with ASD may feel overloaded by input. Compare this concept to a birthday party at the arcade. After being bumped into by a hundred small children, hearing the sirens and wails of the video-games, and watching a group of children run about in utter chaos, one feels as if they might burst from sensory overload. Perhaps a child with ASD has a lower, or different, threshold level for stimulation which may be like living with just such an arcade in his head.

We need to have a heightened awareness of this sensory difference in children with ASD. When they are "losing it," it is not enough to say "He's got to get control of himself." We need to look more closely at what in his environment could be contributing to the overload. Attempting to better understand what it is that he may be experiencing can help one intervene in the most effective manner. It might be as simple as escorting a child out of a crowded room, or teaching a child to turn down the volume on the stereo system and dimming the lights.

Alteration in motor function

Coordination and control

Many children with ASD have a delay in the acquisition of motor skills. They may be somewhat slower than their peers to walk or run, and in many cases when they do start to walk they seem unsteady in their gait. Many parents describe their children as "clumsy." "They don't seem to know where their body is going," said one father. This delay has been looked at from various points of view and different explanations are given by professionals in the field of developmental pediatrics.

Even simple movements have a complicated brain process behind them. The fine tuning of walking, for example, is under the control of multiple brain motor control centers. These centers control the gradation of movement, balance, muscle tone, and coordination. There are also neurologic centers that are responsible for evaluating the purpose of walking, which entails the social implication of walking. This concept is illustrated when watching boys "strut" down the street, as compared to cheer-leaders who "bounce" as they walk. Our gait, therefore, can be thought of as part of our non-verbal communication. Because the master control mechanism in ASD is frequently tuned differently, it is common to see a combination of awkward movements. To make matters more confusing, the effects are not uniform. Some highly complex motor tasks may be very well-developed, while simple tasks are poorly developed. A child who is able to climb proficiently in the playground, walks up on his toes in a bizarre pattern when in the school hallway.

A second explanation for the alteration in motor skills seen in ASD children is because they are not fully connected to their surroundings. Due to this they have poorer motor planning, or understanding of one's body in space. They are not fully sensing themselves in the space around them as they move about.

A third explanation is, because the basis of ASD lies in the neurochemical or neurostructural functioning of the brain, it is very likely that the brain functions responsible for motor control are also affected. Again, as we learn more about the complicated central control system, we may have a better understanding of the more specific alteration in brain functioning in children with ASD. This will likely help us understand not only the origins of the core deficits, but will also help us better understand the differences in physical movements.

Physical mannerism

Children on the spectrum of ASD are often noted to have unusual movements, or mannerisms. These mannerisms are also referred to as stereotypic movements, as they tend to be repetitive in nature and can involve the whole body or isolated parts. A child will rock or sway rhythmically, another will flap his hands. Facial grimacing and strange vocalizations often go along with the physical movements, or can be seen or heard separately.

Unusual movements and mannerisms can occur spontaneously, or they may be triggered by excitement, boredom, or anxiety. They become predictable movements that are habit-based, that is they are done repeatedly out of habit. Many people have mannerisms due to habit. Thumb sucking is a socially appropriate stereotyped movement seen in infants and small children. Adults may twirl a strand of hair or stroke at a beard repetitively. Individuals with ASD commonly have stereotypic movements that are not appropriate, or considered socially acceptable at a given time or in a given circumstance. Hand flapping, spinning, and head rocking are behaviors often seen in children with ASD that set them apart from their peers.

Children have these mannerisms for a variety of reasons. People are innately calmed, or soothed by rhythmic movements. Sucking, one of our very primitive reflexes, is very much a rhythmic action. Infants are calmed by rocking and swaying motions. This leads us to the notion that it is likely to be for the same reason that children with ASD do this. Furthermore, the fact that many children with ASD are not as aware of what is socially acceptable among their peers or have not fully learned what is an appropriate social reaction, may lead them to respond in this more primitive nature. One mother shared that when watching a soccer game her son would flap his hands so much that he actually scared the other supporters of his team. It finally struck her that this was simply his response to the excitement around him. He was not able to pick up on how the other children were acting in this situation and he was internally driven to express himself in this way. It was, however, distressing to him that the other children were shying away from him, so he and his mother worked together on learning the appropriate response for this situation. His mother actually scripted a response for him to follow when he felt excited, and though it still appeared somewhat stilted in its performance, the boy's new found way of yelling "Go! Go! Yea team!" while clapping was accepted by his peers.

Physical mannerisms are a cause of great concern to many parents as they are an outward sign of the internal difference in the child. Parents often respond to these bizarre looking movements with fear and anxiety. In stepping back from the situation and trying to take a more objective view, a parent may be able to better define what is the trigger for such behavior and come up with an effective plan to help the child be more socially appropriate. Offering an alternative means of expression may change the course of the mannerisms.

Sometimes twitch-like movements or repetitive sounds may occur in children with developmental disabilities. These brief, episodic patterns are called tics. They have a very different origin from mannerisms, though they can be difficult to differentiate. Tics represent small short circuits in the neuromotor functions of the brain. They may worsen in frequency or intensity with excitement, boredom, or anxiety but they are not willful mechanisms, and they serve to calm, sooth, or excite the person. They are involuntary movements and often present initially as eye movements or face twitches. Should such movements occur, it is reasonable to bring them to the attention of a physician. While mannerisms are best managed with behavioral and cognitive interventions, consideration of medical management of tics is made when they are intrusive or obstruct a child from functioning optimally.

Unusual strengths and skills

The development of specific areas of interest or advanced skills, beyond the expected level of competency for a child that age, is another baffling component of the disorder of ASD. This is most commonly seen in children with Asperger syndrome (AS), and it is included in the diagnostic criteria of the disorder. It can also be seen in other children on the spectrum. Yet another finding that is not fully understood, is that children with ASD can reveal unusual presentations of some advanced cognitive skills, unique skill sets, and/or uneven learning profiles. A child with average capabilities is unable to do certain academic subjects, yet excels in other areas. A profile of strengths and weaknesses emerges.

Early reading, or hyperlexia, is a skill children with ASD may possess. This initially presents as early identification of letters and quick memorization of the manner in which a book is read to them. Some children are reading well before they even enter school. The level of oral reading skill often exceeds the comprehension level and when the child is asked more socially loaded questions related to the content of the reading, the child with ASD has difficulty coming up with answers. We spoke to a little girl with AS, Amy, who is five years old and has read the entire series of American Girl stories. These books are at about the third grade reading level and explore the lives of girls growing up in the different eras of American culture. Though Amy was able to tell in great detail the content of the books, she showed no emotional connection to what she had read. When asked how she felt about the girls, or for the girls in the various moments of strife and triumph, Amy was unable to answer and reverted back to reciting various excerpts that had been of interest to her. Amy repetitively reads the books now and enjoys them lined up in the series on her shelves. Though she has not fully understood the content of the stories, the fact that she can read is an incredible strength for her and other children who develop this skill. Because books tend to be so socially and emotionally loaded, they are great tools to use to expand a child's social understanding and emotional response. Stories have the capacity to tap into an area of deficit for the child with ASD and expand on skills.

In addition to hyperlexia, the skills of concrete learning of concrete things also applies to shapes and spatial relations. It is for this reason that high functioning children with ASD will know when their mother has taken a different path to the grocery store and will be able to direct their father to a park he has not been to before. Exceptional spatial concepts can also be illustrated by adeptness for puzzles. It is often reported that a child can do puzzles, which are way beyond the expected age skill level. Because the children have a propensity for these tasks, they tend to like them.

Any preference of play that a child has can then be used and expanded upon to promote growth in areas of weakness. These areas of strength are just that, areas of strength. With the proper education and guidance, a child can use them to expand on their less well-developed areas of communication, and socialization.

The Evaluation Process

Where to start

Perhaps the hardest step in the process of having a child evaluated is the first one: identifying that you need to. Many parents have shared similar stories of their sense that something wasn't "quite right" with their child, and yet were unable to actually put their finger on exactly what it was. Often, due to the limited amount of time that pediatricians and family doctors have to see a young child in the office setting, the problems associated with ASD are not revealed. "Red flags" may go up for some doctors when parents share concerns regarding eye contact, lack of speech and communication efforts, but more subtle differences seen in children more mildly affected on the autism spectrum may not be deemed significant. Peculiarities in play style, singular interests and difficulties with sensory input are just some of the characteristics that may not be highlighted to the physician.

Physicians and professionals working with children have become more familiar with the changes in diagnostic criteria and terminology in the concept of autism as a spectrum. The increased prevalence and awareness of autism spectrum disorder (ASD) and improved appreciation for the profound impact of directed early interventions has led to an increased demand for early developmental evaluations and diagnosis. The demand is perhaps passing the supply in terms of availability of trained specialists equipped to complete thorough and precise evaluations. This has led to the difficulty of an accumulation of parents having concerns about autistic tendencies, and they may have to wait to have their concerns heard and their needs addressed. Measures are underway globally to meet this need and better screening and evaluation tools, increased training for personnel, and public awareness are just some of the influential factors contributing to better early identification of ASD. Additionally, direct screening for autistic characteristics at the 18-month well-child medical visit was initiated by the American Academy of Pediatrics (AAP). Because of this, many children are having earlier referrals to specialists and supports are being initiated in a prompt fashion.

Even with this heightened awareness among the professionals working with children, parent concern often remains the driving force behind further developmental assessment. And, regardless of what concern brought the parent and child to the table, the assessment process may be a trying and difficult experience. Whether it affirms beliefs or denies them, the evaluation process is a challenging one.

Expectations of a diagnosis

Where it was once considered alarming news for most parents to hear news that their child had the developmental profiles of autism spectrum disorder (ASD), it is now not uncommon for parents to seek evaluations specifically for their concerns about what they think are autistic characteristics. It has become increasingly important to identify what is NOT ASD. For example, children who are delayed in speech and language, and are somewhat anxious in social situations may retreat in the social setting with peers. A child with poor attention who is quite active may need time to tune into a new social environment. In both these scenarios, the question of social capability is raised and with it concerns about autism. Skilled practitioners continue to work to clearly define and differentiate developmental disorders accurately.

Finding an evaluator

Referral to an evaluator can be done via a variety of options. First, discuss with your primary doctor your specific concerns and ascertain his or her recommendations on how to proceed. In such a case, medical referral can be made to a developmental pediatrician, neurologist, psychologist, or child psychiatrist. Developmental evaluations may be supported by other professionals as well. Public health offices can direct a parent to a means of evaluation for the young child. Local school districts will be able to direct parents in regard to developmental and educational evaluation for the school-age child. Often evaluations are accomplished by a team of professionals. These teams include combinations of the many professionals including: medical professionals, educational specialists and therapists, and psychologists.

Specialists and roles

Developmental pediatrician: A pediatrician with additional specialized training with a fellowship in developmental pediatrics. The focus of this line of medical practice is on developmental disorders and disabilities.

Child psychiatrist: A medical doctor with specialization in psychiatric and developmental diagnosis. The focus of this line of medical practice is on mental health in children and psychiatric illness.

Pediatric neurologist: A doctor with specialization in neurologic conditions. The focus of this line of medical practice is on neurologic functioning and disease processes of the brain and nervous system.

Developmental nurse: A nurse with further training and experience in child development.

Speech pathologist: A Master's prepared professional with expertise in speech and language.

Special educator: A teacher trained to work with children with special needs.

Social worker: An individual with a Master's degree in social work.

Physical therapist: An individual trained to work with motor needs of children.

Occupational therapist: An individual trained in working with use of hands and functional skills of daily living.

Psychologist: An individual trained in clinical psychology, developmental psychology, school psychology, or related degree.

Because parents going to the evaluation may not yet know the specific diagnostic concerns they are facing, it can be hard to hand-pick who would best serve them. Parents should rely on the professionals they trust to guide them.

Regardless of who the evaluation is completed by, parents should feel comfortable with how the evaluation went and have confidence in the professionals who are in the position of diagnosing and determining their child's needs. We would encourage parents to seek out further information through second opinions, reading material and from other parents, if they feel the need.

What to expect from the evaluation process

Depending on the background of the examiner, or team, the process of the evaluation will vary. The tools used, or the developmental tests and materials worked from, will vary. There are also some tools designed more specifically for the area of autism that may be useful. An important point to note, however, is that the nature of ASD is such that the diagnosis is made by the appreciation of the qualitative differences in the areas of communication and especially social relatedness. This is accomplished often through the level of experience and established level of expertise of the examiner. In a good evaluation, the examiners are able to get a thorough and complete medical, developmental and genetic history; observe play, socialization, and problem solving tasks; have direct interaction between child and examiner; and conduct some cognitive skill level testing to get a sense of the child's level of intelligence. It is often difficult to achieve the latter of these, as children with ASD do not always reveal their true cognitive, or problem solving, abilities in a test format. Tools to better assess cognition in light of language difficulties are evolving and better information can be obtained from these if additional concerns regarding cognitive capability are raised. A neurologic motor examination is also helpful in differentiating multiple potential diagnosis.

The developmental history, or story about how the child has progressed, is very important as it is often the nature of developmental progress that illuminates the difference in the style of development in the child with ASD. A child having language and then losing it, or the child having the ability to recite a commercial he has seen, but not being able to ask for juice, are peculiarities in the course of development that may not be revealed by standardized testing, but rather by developmental anecdote.

Furthermore, a child's degree of connectedness is something that is more observable than testable. It is difficult to quantify, or objectively give a score or value to the presentation of this area of impairment. The examiners rely on their understanding of normal development, knowledge of the characteristics of ASD and overall experience to recognize the disorder.

The length of the evaluation process then is not always directly related to an accurate evaluation. It is difficult for some parents to accept that such a diagnosis can be made after a professional has only spent limited time with the child. Again, it is the appreciation for the areas of impairment and level of expertise with this population that influences the accuracy of the diagnosis.

Physical examination and medical work-up

Any time one is looking at development, the child's physical and health status needs to be taken into account. A medical history and a brief physical examination should be performed. The examination is usually unremarkable, in that children with ASD tend not to have physical differences. There are a few other diagnoses that may need to be ruled out, however, and these may be taken note of on physical examination. An examiner will look for dysmorphisms, or unusual differences in physical appearance. Facial features, hands and fingers, as well as other body parts, may point to a genetic syndrome or condition. On physical examination, children with ASD may have a large head size, although this does not necessarily point to a structural difference in the brain itself.

Medical testing

"Can't you run a blood test to know for sure?" was the plea of one mother in need of medical confirmation to accept the diagnosis. Unfortunately, the answer to that question is "no". Currently, no medical testing can confirm the diagnosis of ASD, but some testing may be indicated and ordered by your physician.

Blood tests

Blood tests require the drawing of blood from the vein of the child. It is then analyzed in the laboratory. For example, there is a genetic condition known as fragile X (addressed later), which can be detected by molecular DNA testing. This looks at the genetic "blue prints" of the child and, while this cannot be altered by any medical intervention, it may assist with diagnosis and is information that may be important in terms of family planning for other family members. Genetic testing has become much more sophisticated and higher levels of gene analysis are being made available. This may lead us to more specified testing in the future for autism. Currently, there is no standard "marker" or specific genetic analysis for autism to confirm diagnosis and/or guide treatment. Blood work and urine tests may also be looked at for metabolic conditions. These are uncommon in children with ASD.

MRI

An MRI, or magnetic resonance imaging, is a means of looking at the brain structure. It entails placing the child on a stretcher, requiring restraint and/or sedation because he has to lie absolutely still, and wheeling him into a large cylinder. Pictures of cross-sections of the brain are taken and they are read by specialists in radiology. This is a costly test that also has a low yield, meaning that it is rare to see a major difference in the brain structure of a child with ASD. Remember again that the difference in the brain may be on a circuitry level, not structural. Lastly, nothing can be done to change the established structure of the brain. It is for all these reasons that MRIs may not be done on children with ASD for the purpose of diagnosis. Parents have a hard time understanding this, perhaps because they are seeking some tangible, clinical indicator of the disorder.

EEG

Another test that may be done on a child with ASD is an EEG, or electroencephalogram. This test entails placing electrodes with a gel-like substance on the surface of the child's head. There are many electrodes to place and, though it is helpful to have the child awake but sleepy for the procedure, it is difficult. There is important information gathered on this study as a child falls to sleep and during their sleep. Given the nature of the test process, it is difficult to get the child to sleep and therefore we are not able to obtain this piece of information from the EEG. The purpose of this test is to look at the electrical wave patterns of the brain. It is designed to look for seizure patterns. This test may be ordered on a child with ASD if there is any indication that a child is having spells that may be actual seizures. It is helpful to do the study because there are medications available for seizures and treating them effectively is important to a child's health and development. It is also relevant to get an EEG if there has been a developmental presentation of a marked fall-off of speech and language skills that had been acquired. This regressive pattern may represent undetected seizures that could be underlying the developmental differences. Fall-off of skill set may also just be representative of the presentation of ASD.

Can other conditions look like ASD?

Laundau Kleffner syndrome is a seizure disorder that can be mistaken for ASD and autism. Children lose their ability to speak due to changes in the electrical patterns of the brain. It generally occurs in older preschool children and is uncommon. It is diagnosed by completion of an EEG. Some medical treatments have proven helpful to children with Laundau Kleffner syndrome (Lewine *et al.* 1999).

Fragile X syndrome, mentioned earlier, is a chromosomal syndrome consisting of a constellation of physical differences including: large head, cupped ears, altered hairline, large body size, poor learning capacity with high rates of mental retardation, poor language development, and social disconnection. This can overlap with ASD.

Can we avoid labeling?

No parent wants a child to carry a label that he or she thinks will stigmatize their child throughout the school years and perhaps beyond. The label should be used to support the parent and child in establishing that there is a biological difference in this child, which is causing the differences in development. In other words, poor parenting, or just being a "bad kid" are not the cause of the child's difficulties. The label should be used to help specify the areas that need to be addressed vigorously. The label should be used to help elevate the child to a better place, not to diminish him. The label should help get the child what he needs. It would be untrue if we said that all professionals, educators and people in a child's world are going to fully accept the child with an open mind and not carry preconceived notions of what it is to be autistic, or to have ASD. Parents are forced to take on the role of educating others as to what the diagnosis means, and more specifically, what it means to their special child: what strengths and weaknesses they bring to the playground, back yard and classroom. Issues that go along with the concept of labeling a child are changing as society is changing. Acceptance of differences in schools and communities is certainly improving over time, and, with every child who has ASD who grows and makes a contribution to the world by being a part of it, the misconceptions will improve.

What Can Be Done? Medical Perspective

Much can be done for children with autism spectrum disorder (ASD). This chapter and the next will look at the medical and educational perspectives. We touch on some key components and intervention modalities, but this is certainly not intended to be inclusive of all methods of testing or intervening. Nor is it all inclusive of the multiple opinions of professionals in the field.

Given the inherent differences in the fields of medicine and education, the focus of moving forward as we have experienced this boom in autism is very different for the two fields. It has become increasingly more important for the worlds to merge and interface as we continue to look forward for children with ASD. The pediatric medical world has responded to the increasing numbers of children identified with autistic characteristics with prompt investigation of prevalence, increased routine developmental assessment at targeted ages, and ongoing professional communication of results of medical research and relevant input. Medical research has been expansive looking at potential environmental factors, genetic factors, and the influence of one on the other. Medical testing procedures and possible medical treatment are utilized and continue to be assessed to determine helpfulness. On the education front, intervention strategies continue to evolve and the high standards used for several years continue to provide the much needed support and education for children with ASD. Additionally, interventions and specialized programs are being looked at closely in terms of what is the outcome for children who utilize a given method, intervention, or attend a given program. This outcome-based assessment is helping us to better define appropriate interventions and program methods.

It is critical that we look at the individual needs both when considering potential medical or educational interventions. Whether a doctor is recommending a given medical test or a teacher is recommending a particular intervention strategy, the profile and needs of the child are highly individual and vary significantly. One child may benefit from the diagnostic study of an electroencephalogram (EEG) while it would be a lot for another to go through for no significant reason. One child may benefit from using pictures to identify needs and initiate communication, while another child may be better served with verbal coaching.

A medical perspective

Having a clear understanding of the struggles that the individual child faces is a huge first step. We are then able to most effectively work with him. Even though the diagnosis of ASD is hard to hear, it is the first step toward the most helpful and appropriate treatment options. Accuracy and specificity of diagnosis is important as then treatment and intervention follows in a more targeted approach. For example if a child has a rash, it is important to know if it is caused by an infection or an allergy. Knowing the difference targets our treatment. One may require an antibiotic, while the other may resolve with a cream. The same is true in treatments for autism and pervasive development disorder (PDD). Being very specific in understanding the underlying problem, and its individualized presentations, may lead to very different approaches to intervention. For example, should a child be delayed in his speech, interventions would be focused on production of words. A child is coached to label their world: "cookie, light, Sissy." However, when a child is socially disconnected in his communication, strategies are implemented to address the attempt at social connection. Pictures, gestures, and sometimes spoken words, are encouraged to help the child make that very important communication piece, social connection.

Medication issues

There is currently no medical cure for any PDD, including the spectrum of autism. There is no pill or treatment that medicinally treats the underlying difficulties.

Research in the field of psychopharmacology has led to a boom in the treatment of many psychiatric and emotional disorders that accompany autism. Also, more is being researched and understood about the chemical and physiological processes of the brain every day. It is likely that significant advances in biologic interventions will take place in the future. At this point, however, there is no direct treatment for autism. All we can do is treat problem symptoms such as anxiety or aggressive behaviors. Remember that many medications used for children with autism are "off label." They have not had the rigorous testing in children to obtain the complete safety and benefits data to allow the United States Food and Drug Administration (FDA) to conclusively approve their use in children. These medications may indeed be safe and useful, but the burden of proof remains for many of them. Careful consideration is important when a child is being placed on such powerful medications.

Though the disorder as a whole cannot currently be treated with medications, many of the complicating factors or co-existing conditions can be managed effectively with medications. As mentioned in the previous chapter, several of the secondary issues may respond well to medication management. It is felt that even though we cannot directly treat the underlying cause, medications can be useful in some children with ASD in an attempt to peel away the layers of various difficulties. In this onion peel approach to medication management, we look to eliminate some of the most significant struggles and issues, in the hopes of optimizing strengths and promoting learning and social development. For example, if a child is so motor driven that he is unable to sit and focus for any productive period of time, it may be helpful to take the edge off the hyperactivity. Perhaps then, educators, parents and therapists can have a more powerful influence on that child. In the same way, if a child gets stuck on a thought or a repetitive behavior, it may be helpful to treat the obsession so that the child is freed up to work on functional skills.

Another issue that can be treated with medication is mood stabilization. Often children with ASD swing through periods of highs and lows. They may experience periods of being more tuned in and periods of being more tuned out. They may have periods of escalated anxiety alternating with calmer times. Often the downside of a mood is represented in children very differently than in adults. When adults experience more depressive moods, they may appear fatigued, withdrawn, and perhaps less expressive. In children, depression is often expressed by periods of agitation. This can be accompanied by increased activity levels, decreased desire to sleep and heightened expressiveness. When we talk about moods fluctuating in adults we visualize mood swinging from the very active to the withdrawn. In children we can see moods fluctuate from the very active to the active and aggressive or agitated. These mood fluctuations can be a considerable source of distress and specific medications may prove to be helpful.

When thinking about starting any child on a medication, several things need to be taken into account. Every medication intervention carries with it inherent risks of side-effects and the pros and cons of any medication for a given child need to be looked at carefully by the prescribing doctor and parents. It is necessary for the parents to have a good handle on the child's behavior prior to the medication trial so they will be able to record and evaluate the child's response to it. They need to be able to accurately communicate changes, side-effects, and/or benefits to the physician. The doctor may prescribe the medication, but the parent is the one who is living with the child. Parents are truly the experts in regard to their child's behaviors. It certainly takes a qualified medical professional to manage a new medication for a child with ASD, and it is for this reason that often a child psychiatrist, child neurologist, or developmental pediatrician is consulted in these matters. Sometimes, family doctors and pediatricians are comfortable prescribing more commonly used drugs, but in other cases they may refer a family for further professional input.

Before starting any medication

Before starting any medication, it must be clear exactly what is being treated. For example, it must be determined whether Julie's circling the living room repeatedly is related to hyperactivity or an expression of anxiety, in order to most specifically treat the problem. This can be achieved by looking closely at a behavior over time. Taking notes and keeping a journal are very useful tools to help define and isolate behaviors. It is important to look at what had been happening before the behavior, what might have triggered the behavior, or what might be precipitating factors. Keeping a journal can help a parent sort this out. If Kristen consistently rocks excessively before getting on the school bus and before going to her grandmother's house it may be more a product of anxiety than hyperactivity. But if she randomly runs in the yard at a neighbor's, that may be more a component of hyperactivity.

Before starting medication, it also must be determined if the behavior being targeted is indeed impairing the child to any significant degree. Is the hyperactivity preventing the child from being able to sit and focus? Is the anxiety blocking his ability to work on social skills? It is also reasonable to think about how the child is co-existing in a family, when deciding if a medication trial is appropriate. If the child is so obsessive that the family can't get through a decent meal because the child has to repeatedly touch his fork and then his knife, it can wreak havoc on family life. That's not to say the physician should medicate a child because the family can't get through a meal. Rather it makes the point that the overall influence that the child's peculiarities are having on the family and their life in general, should be taken into account.

At what point to start medication is determined by the physician and the parents. Parents should feel comfortable with the decision and have confidence in the expertise of their doctor. Parents will need to be in contact with the doctor to let him or her know of the child's response and to make any adjustments that are indicated by the physician. Medication should not be stopped abruptly without notifying the physician, as some medications have to be weaned, or reduced gradually.

If the child is old enough and able to understand, it is important that the child is part of the decision-making process. They need to know why a medication is going to be started and what they will need to tell their parents about if they experience side-effects. They may be fearful of a medication if they do not know what to expect from it. They need to know that the medication is supposed to help them in a certain area and why changing that would be helpful to them.

All trials of medication are just that, trials. If a medication is started and it does not provide the desired response, or if side-effects emerge, it can be stopped. Finding the right medication, in the right amount, for the right child, can be a process of trial and error. Sometimes, a particular medication may not work well for a very young child, but when tried at an older age it is effective. Therefore, parents should not feel that if a medication does not work at one point they should never try that medication, or others, again.

It is important to know what side-effects to look for with any given drug. Journal keeping can be helpful in gathering the information into meaningful terms. For example, if meals are recorded, it is easy to see if appetite has waned during a medication trial. If not written down, it may be difficult to recall small changes over time.

Some considerations when journaling/documenting medication response:

- Record keeping should occur before and after initiation of a medication. Consistency of record keeping is important even if "things look good" is reported from the teacher. Look for appropriate support at school, such as school nurses or school psychologists.

- Include sleep information: time in bed to time asleep, length of sleep, arousals during night, periods of restlessness, child's ability to arouse in morning, fatigue during day, napping or dozing during day.

- Include appetite information: schedule of meals/snacks, items desired/eaten, volume of food consumed, onset in cravings, places food eaten.

- Target symptom being treated and set up documentation around given symptom; that is, if hyperactivity is being addressed look specifically at how the child presents hyperactivity and record frequency, intensity and duration. For example, won't sit in circle time and circles classroom. Record what the activity level is, scale it for severity, and how long it lasts. Another example: has to repeat washing hands in pattern. Record what behavior is, how long it lasts, when it occurs and what stops it.

- Record agitation or periods of emotionality. Does the child seem weepy or "out of sorts"?

- Track weight and growth.

- Document any unusual movements, tremors, or things you find different about your child.

Usage of medications

This review is intended to be only a brief look at some more commonly used medications. It is by no means all inclusive of the many medications currently available. Additionally, if one of these medications is used for a child, the parent should get further specific information regarding the drug from his or her doctor and/or pharmacist. Any side-effects should be reported to your doctor. All medications should be taken as directed.

Medication to treat agitation/aggression

ATYPICAL ANTI-PSYCHOTICS

Now FDA approved for symptoms associated with autism. Risperidone (Risperdal) and aripiprazole (Abilify).

Desired effect: Decrease in state of agitation and/or aggression.

Method of administration: Given by mouth. Must be taken at regular intervals and it is important to follow prescription directions. These medications cannot be stopped abruptly as may cause worsened agitation and confusion. It may take a few weeks to see positive effects of these medications.

Side-effects: Increase in appetite and weight gain (worse for risperidone). May see initially some irritability. Headache, nausea, constipation, fatigue, change in saliva production, and trouble sleeping. Rarely, muscle ache and pains are reported.

Attention/impulse control
PSYCHOSTIMULANT DRUGS
The most common treatment of attention/impulse control symptoms are stimulant drugs, which improve focus, sustained attention, and motoric restlessness. Methylphenidate-based (Ritalin, Concerta), dexmethyphenidate (modified methyphenidate-focalin), dextroamphetamine-based (Dexedrine, Adderal), lisdesamfetamin (Vyvanse).

Desired effect: Decrease in activity, increase in attentiveness.

Method of administration: Given by mouth. These medications come in short-acting and long-acting compounds. Some may require administration at school or other settings outside the home.

Side-effects: Vary among compounds and release mechanisms. Generally common side-effects include: loss of appetite, nausea, headache, difficulty sleeping, agitation, and "rebound" (worsened behaviors as the drug is wearing off).

Hyperactivity (standing alone)
ALPHA BLOCKING AGENTS
1. Clonodine (Catapres).

Desired effect: Decreased hyperactivity, decreased aimless excessive energy.

Method of administration: Commonly given in a patch form so that the medication is absorbed over time. The patch only has to be put on every few days and therefore this drug doesn't require frequent administration. Clonodine also can be given in pill form by mouth.

Side-effects: Local irritation at the site of the patch. Some children do not like the feel of the patch on their skin. Significant sedation can occur. Lowering of blood pressure may occur. This medication may not be stopped abruptly.

2. Guanfacine (Tenex).

Desired effect: Decreased hyperactivity, decreased aimless excessive energy.

Method of administration: Given by mouth and require a few doses over the course of the day. Needs to be titrated up to desired dose.

Side-effects: Fatigue, irritability when first on medication. Constipation, nausea, and more rarely complaints of muscle weakness and aches. May lower blood pressure.

Anxiety and obsessive compulsive disorder (OCD)
ANTIDEPRESSANTS/ANXIOLITICS
Selective serotonin reuptake inhibitors (SSRIs) are the drugs of choice for this disorder, along with different types of antidepressants: Fluoxetine hydrochloride (Prozac), sertraline (Zoloft), fluvoxamine maleate (Luvox), clomipramine (Anafranil), escitalopram (Lexapro).

Also, miscellaneous antidepressants/anxiolitics: busproprion (Wellbutrin), busperone (BusPar).

Desired effect: Decrease in obsessive compulsive tendencies, anxiety response, and/or treatment of depression.

Method of administration: Given in pill form by mouth.

Side-effects: Increased anxiety, agitation, nausea, vomiting, headaches, worsened hyperactive behavior, loss of appetite and sleep difficulties.

Severe episodic anxiety

In some situations short-acting anti-anxiety medications are helpful, such as prior to procedures, for example if dentistry causes a child severe anxiety and resultant acting out. Medical procedures can be very trying, particularly if the child has been through the given test before and has established anxiety around it and/or they have fear of doctors' offices or hospitals.

The following may be helpful: benzodiazepines; lorazapam (Ativan), clorazepam (Klonopin), diazepam (Valium).

Side-effects: Sedation, nausea, confusion, agitation.

Special consideration: These medications should be considered only when targeted anxiety-provoking episodes are identified.

Mood stabilization

If there is a strong family history of bipolar disorder (manic depressive disorder) or depression, a doctor may be more inclined to think that a child may be struggling with a problem of mood. In such cases, and others that seem to manifest fluctuations in moods, mood stabilizers, especially anticonvulsants, may be used. Originally designed for the treatment of seizure activity, these drugs have also been helpful in treating ASD children. They have been around for a long time and they have been used with children for a long time, so they are deemed reasonably safe in the pediatric population. Newer versions have proven to be quite helpful and have fewer long-term side-effects.

Anticonvulsants

1. Lamotrigine (Lamictal), oxcarbazine (Trileptal).

Method of administration: Given by mouth. Dosing is carefully titrated up to target dose over several weeks. Adherence to administration regime is critical as rapid administration has significant side-effects.

Desired effects: Calm the child, even out moods, and suppress extremes in excitation/agitation.

Side-effects: diarrhea, constipation, sleeping difficulty, headache, nausea, and tremor. It is critical to administer as directed as a lethal rash has been associated with these medications when they are titrated too quickly or given in too high a dose. Any rash should be immediately reported to the child's physician.

2. Carbamazepine (Tegretol), valproate (Depakene, Depakote).

Method of administration: Given in pill form by mouth.

Desired effect: Calm the child, prevent and treat mood swings, especially over-excitement.

These drugs require a certain level in the blood to be effective. Therefore, blood may need to be sampled on occasion to make sure that it is in the right quantity in the child's blood system. If the level is too low the drug may not be working. If the level is too high the child may have unwanted effects such as staggered gait and clumsy walking.

Side-effects: Vomiting, abdominal pain, unsteadiness.

What Can Be Done? Educational Perspective

This chapter will look at a few of the modalities of teaching that are predominantly used today. It will give some guidelines for determining what therapist and/or program will meet an individual child's needs. Hopefully, this will help you answer for yourselves: "Where do we go from here?"

The logical next step following the diagnosis is seeking appropriate interventions and education for a child with ASD. There are many good programs and many dedicated people working with these children. They are committed to making a difference and they surely do. However, this remains a confusing and sometimes overwhelming time for parents as they are in the throws of just beginning to understand what the diagnosis means, and trying to accept the implications that it has on their child and their family. In the midst of this, they are challenged with the task of learning about the multitude of modalities of teaching children with autism spectrum disorder (ASD), selecting the best option for their child, and finding therapists and/or a program. This is quite a project and takes a great deal of effort, but there are people who can support parents through the process.

Getting started

There truly is something for everyone out there. An alphabet soup of educational terms and an array of theorists result in a diverse selection of educational opportunities for children with ASD. While evaluators can help guide families by clearly defining the child's areas of need, parents are truly at the helm of the decision-making process in regards to implementation of servicing. The first step is for the parent to get informed as to what the various modalities entail and what is available. They may find it helpful to obtain the support of professionals in their region or area to assist in this process. Offices of primary doctors, early intervention, public health departments or school departments of special education may be good places to seek out such support.

It is not uncommon for a parent to read of a very specific teaching strategy for children with ASD only to find that they do not have access to a program or therapist with training in this particular method. Often, "variations on a theme" so to speak are available and with good research, parents are usually able to find the appropriate intervention available to their child. Parents should meet with therapists, go to see programs in action and discuss the child's individual needs. They should determine how a given therapist or program would address these needs. Parents have shared that they generally ended up with a "gut feeling" about what was the right thing to do. It can often be the trained specialist who "clicks" with a given child and has multiple options to implement in the educational process, that has the greatest impact on that child. While strategies and modalities are certainly important in providing a framework for intervention, we encourage parents not to feel that they have to take only one way to education. It can be hard to know from the outset what methods will be most effective for a child. Again, parents should be informed as to what has worked for other children with ASD and what is available to them. They are then in a better position to make a sound decision.

This brings up another important point. What if a parent does not find anything in their area that they think supports an appropriate education plan for their child? The parent now is in the position of advocating for implementation of such a program, or training. We advise that if such is the situation, a parent should obtain valid research and published information on the modality that they are trying to have implemented, and present it to the persons in their area who are in control of programming issues. This may be a person in an early intervention office or someone at the school district. Professionals in the field of child development are often open to furthering their own educational background, and/or trying out new strategies or methods. It might just be an issue of setting up the appropriate means of educating the people who would be working with the child with ASD. Due to expansion of diagnostic terminology in this field and the increasing number of children being diagnosed, it has been our experience that therapists and teachers are very interested in expanding their skills in this area.

Another issue of concern in determining the best intervention options for a child with ASD has to do with intensity of servicing. Due to the great need for intensive socialization and communication intervention, these children often benefit from special schools and programs. This is true even for children as young as two-and-a-half to three years. It has been felt in the past that young children benefit from working in the familiar environment of their home. This can be a good place to start, certainly if a child needs some time to become familiar with therapists, to be able to comfortably work with them. It can also be very helpful to establish some basic skill sets before having to acclimate to an unfamiliar social setting. It has to be noted, however, that it is most beneficial to immerse the child with ASD into the more social context of a special classroom, or integrated program, to optimize opportunities to work on socialization and communication. It is heart-wrenching for some to send a toddler off to a school, but we need to emphasize that the one thing that we are sure of for children with ASD is that the earlier and more intensively we directly work on the areas of impairment, the more likely it is that the child will have significant adaptation to the developmental disorder. To optimize school-age placement with minimal support, much work needs to be accomplished for all children with ASD, regardless of where they fall along the spectrum. Decisions regarding where and what interventions will be implemented also depend on the age at which the child is diagnosed. It may be reasonable to start a very young child with intervention in the home setting to acclimatize both the child and the parents to the educational process.

While in the case of the child first diagnosed at more than three years of age, it is almost always indicated to place the child into a center-based program.

How to proceed

First, parents need to familiarize themselves with the roles of the different therapists, and the various educational modalities and intervention methods. We will look at some of the most common modalities. When reviewing your child's options specifically, it will be important to seek further reference material for the given methods and interventions. It is important to meet with potential therapists, and visit programs using various methods and see exactly what they do day-to-day. Even if a program says it follows a certain method, there is so much variability in the way that programs are implementing these techniques, that the actual programs are very different. For instance, two programs that use applied behavioral analysis (ABA) may actually look very different in practice. Also, two speech therapists may have very different styles and/or teaching strategies within the same framework of speech and language therapy.

Roles of related services

A diverse group of educators and therapists work with children on the autism spectrum. Each area of expertise focuses on given areas, but all take into account the multifaceted nature of children. For example, one cannot work exclusively on the area of speech and language development without taking into account the child's play and learning style. Additionally, within a group of therapists of a particular orientation, there is variability in methods of practice, techniques used, levels of experience and personality characteristics. All these factors influence the effectiveness of the interventions employed.

Speech therapy is a cornerstone of intervention for most children with ASD due to their needs in the area of speech and language. The role of the speech therapist in this population is important not only in helping the child with the production of words and understanding of language, but more importantly, in helping the child understand the power and process of communication. Speech therapists are trained professionals with an advanced degree in speech and language pathology. They use a variety of methods to facilitate the development of language and conversational skills.

Special educators are teachers trained to work with children who have special needs. Levels of preparation vary from associate degrees to those with graduate degrees. The approaches and techniques vary from one therapist to another depending on their training and experiences. Special educators can be very important to the child with ASD in their effort to promote socialization skills, establish more productive and useful play skills, and to fill in the gaps in scattered learning skills. They also help with the expansion of communication skills.

Physical therapists focus on the gross motor area, or area of motor control of the whole body. They are versed in the expected body movements of children and work to establish appropriate movement and physical skill. Because some children with ASD have differences in their body movement and coordination, physical therapists may be helpful.

Occupational therapists work with fine motor, or hand usage, as well as an array of self-help skills. Children with ASD often have difficulty controlling their fingers and hands to do effective writing, cutting, use of eating utensils, and such. Occupational therapists also work to develop appropriate activities of daily living skills, such as dressing. Some occupational therapists have a particular interest and expertise with children with ASD and focus on the child's response to sensory input. They may be able to help with the child's response or aversion to certain feelings on their skin, called tactile defensiveness. The term 'sensory integration' means different things to different people, but in this context, it is used to mean the efforts that a therapist will put into helping the child receive sensory input, tolerate it and make sense of it.

Social work and psychology are related services that play an important role in the child with ASD's intervention plan. These specialists work with the child to help with behaviors and social skills. Some design behavior modification plans to eliminate unwanted behaviors or foster desired behaviors. Social workers and psychologists can also help with social skill training. Parents often benefit from the guidance and support of these professionals, and, particularly for older children with ASD, it is important that they have a professional to help them work through feelings of insecurity, alienation, and possibly depression.

Methods of educational intervention

Special education

Trained special educators work directly with children in individual and groups setting. These specialists work in teams with speech and language pathologists, occupational therapists and other skilled child development specialists. Their methods vary and often teaching is accomplished through play. Various teaching strategies are used with toys and play schemes to expand on the child's view of the world and to develop skills. Toys are generally representative of the real world and, therefore, are inherently useful tools in expanding a child's repertoire. Play is not random in therapy sessions, but rather it is directed by the skilled therapist to foster development of the specific skills associated with a child's social world. The effective therapist focuses specifically on the child's individual existing repertoire and expands to meet their greater needs.

When watching some special education methods in action, parents may think that all the therapist is actually doing is playing with the child. This method really does require a great deal of expertise, however, when done correctly to yield the desired learning and play skill development. When left to their own devices, most children with ASD will be quite limited in their style of play and area of interest. It does not benefit them to be stuck in limited play schemes. They need to be directed and led to expand on their play. Teaching needs to be in a systematic and thoughtful manner under the guidance of an experienced therapist. In effective play therapy sessions the environment is structured to eliminate distractions and encourage attraction to desired items. The teacher continuously engages the child. The teacher, or child, initiates the play and the teacher then promotes elaboration and expansion of the play schemes. Evaluation of progress is essential and feedback results in modifications in programming. Specific goals are set and advanced when a skill set is acquired. If goals are not set in predetermined time, revisions to the plan are made.

It is important to recognize that many approaches have a positive impact on children on the spectrum of autism. While it is very difficult to ascertain the direct impact of any given approach, it is important to attempt to seek intervention that is supported by evidence-based results. This means that the intervention being utilized with a child has been found to be successful on other children. Some forms of intervention lend themselves to this concept of evidence-based therapy better than others. For example, ABA approaches include vigilant data keeping of a child's response to a specific task. This allows for collection of data that readily identifies change over time. This methodology has been shown to be successful and is supported by evidence. Many methods, or models of intervention are coming forth with evidence-based results. In other words, children are demonstrating tremendous gains from many methods of intervention. Accumulating such evidence is, however, not such a straightforward process. Some methods are attempting to site positive results but are not as data driven and, therefore, it is harder to accumulate substantial information documenting change over time. Better methods of assessment and heightened awareness of need for such documentation has led to a movement of improved methods. This will likely be met with many more approaches being able to offer what is considered evidence that their system of intervention indeed works. It is necessary for parents to discuss this issue with providers of intervention services and school programs to best understand what methods are used and what has been the results seen in the programs. Parents are then challenged to determine if these results are substantiated. Many issues are at play when seeking appropriate intervention.

A key point is that the actual therapist is as important as the modality. Good therapists know how to get the desired response from a child and they can work wonders. As discussed in previous chapters, play is a very important pathway in understanding the social world that we live in. Play in this respect is often limited in even the higher functioning children with ASD. Play skills need to be worked on for every child with ASD in a supported, structured way.

The individuality of all children points us to a need for interventions and programming that meet those individual needs. Blended programming, or the implementation of various methods and approaches, or "variations on a theme", allow us to utilize relevant pieces of many methods to optimize our connection and work with a child.

Use of structured behavioral approaches

The field of behaviorism has been around for a very long time and has been helpful in many teaching opportunities. Essentially the idea is that people are motivated by reinforcement. We like rewards and are motivated to do things we would not otherwise do if a reward awaits us. Many reinforcement models have been utilized for children with ASD. Token systems, sticker charts, and even just praise can be put into many interventions to move children forward by motivating them to accomplish a task. When children are not naturally motivated to accomplish a new skill set, it can be helpful to set up a system of reinforcement that stimulates them to be engaged in the new learning task.

Behavior modification

Maladaptive behaviors can be effectively modified by well-designed systems that look at what sets off a behavior, defines the actual nature of the behavior, and evaluates what occurs after the behavior. Examining this sequence of events can lead us to some conclusions about what is motivating and/or causing a behavior. We can then modify the contributing factors to alter the behavior. And, when that modification is successfully accomplished by the child, it is reinforced. Behavior modification programs require good observation and documentation, articulation of a plan, and implementation of that plan. Revisions are made as the tasks are accomplished. Often, skilled professionals are asked to assist with the formulation of a behavior modification plan. These are usually accomplished around a specific problem area or specific maladaptive behavior.

Applied behavioral analysis (ABA)

ABA became a popular methodology for working with children on the autistic spectrum several years ago. The grassroots of behaviorism, however, its broader term, have been around for decades. Specific methods employing the ABA technique were implemented with increased intensity and time allotment for young children with ASD. This approach came from an advocate for intensive application of ABA among the pervasive development disorder (PDD) population, O. Ivar Lovaas (Maurice, Green and Luce 1996). There is good scientific evidence that this rather intensive approach has been helpful in making meaningful changes in many but not all children with autism.

ABA is a methodology that uses specific training session. These discrete trials are one-on-one instruction in which the teacher prompts a desired response (done in a variety of ways), the child gives the response and gets a reward, or reinforcement. A reward can simply be praise or a small token. If the child does not give the desired behavior, some programs give no response, some give negative reinforcement (not popular among most parents), and some correct the response.

Discrete trials are used to accomplish specific simple tasks, such as consistently looking at someone in the face. "Look at me!" has become the mantra of many parents. When more complicated skills need to be mastered, they are broken down into smaller, simpler pieces and trained one by one in this format. Eventually, these simple components are strung together into a more meaningful whole

The amount of time spent in discrete trial is dependent on the given program. Some therapists and/or programs spend short periods of 5–10 minutes every hour, while others spend 30 minutes –1 hour, five times a day. Some do discrete trials in a separate confined space while others are found prompting a response and giving a reward in the middle of "circle time". No two programs apply this method in the same fashion.

ABA begins with observation and analysis of a behavior, or skill, over time. The task at hand is then broken down into smaller parts and those parts are then taught singularly with each success being rewarded. These small pieces are then strung together until the child has acquired the new skill or task. A cornerstone to this method of teaching is the ongoing recording and evaluation of the responses. Constant modifications in the methods need to be applied. While parents can learn this technique and do it on their own, it is helpful to have the guidance and experience of someone familiar with the techniques in order for its application to be most effective.

Every child who receives intervention through the modality of ABA does not necessarily need discrete trial training. The higher functioning children with ASD may have already mastered many simple tasks taught in the discrete trial setting and intervention time may be more wisely spent in social group settings. Again, ABA programs implement the use of discrete trial training and methods of behaviorism in different ways.

Regardless of all the controversial issues surrounding its usage, and inconsistent application of the method, ABA can be a strong strategy for teaching skills and changing behaviors. It is for this reason that parents should familiarize themselves with the basics of ABA, whether they choose it as the primary modality for their child or not. It can be a useful component to any individual plan, and for some children, modified use in a more natural setting can be very beneficial. It might not take hours sitting across from a trained teacher for some children with ASD to "look at me" but implementing the reward system component of ABA in the classroom may be a useful tool. Conversely, a more severely involved child with no eye contact may require multiple discrete trials before they will meet your eyes. Any, and all, approaches need to be individualized to the given child's specific needs.

An issue that must be addressed when working in the framework of ABA is generalization. Generalization is the ability to take what is learned in one setting and apply it consistently in other situations. Children with ASD have a very difficult time with this, as they are often concrete learners and the carry-over of skills is hard for them in different settings. A child sitting across the table from a teacher in a discrete trial can say, "Hello, my name is Sally." This isn't useful in the bigger scheme of things if the child is not able to do it anywhere else. Efforts to foster generalization have increased as awareness of its importance has come to the forefront. Establishing the functional use of skills has got to be a key focus of any intervention strategy.

Consistency of training among many people in the child's world, as well as applying the basic techniques in everyday living, are important means of promoting generalization.

Social adaptation intervention methods

An effective means of interacting and intervening with children with ASD has been found to be by social adaptation. Taking the view of the primary struggle being social difficulties, these approaches focus specifically on fostering growth through helping the child learn a means to adapt and socially connect. Various programs utilize this concept. A sample of one such program is "The treatment and education of autistic and related communication handicapped children" (TEACCH) (Mesibov 1994). Techniques employed by this program are being successfully implemented in many other programs and utilized by therapists.

The TEACCH program sets up structured educational environments to encourage skill development in specific areas of impairment. Individual assessment and programming occur with a focus on communication and socialization training. Children are observed at length to establish a baseline of skills. Communication skills, both verbal and non-verbal, are then built upon. ASD is viewed as a multidimensional variation in development and teaching methods are designed to cross that multidimension. Generalization is a priority, and parents play a large role in fostering it by keeping abreast of what is being implemented in the classroom and bringing those strategies to the home setting.

Structure and routine are cornerstones of this method. Also, learning is fostered with many visual cues. Children with ASD are not usually auditory learners. In other words, it is hard for them to learn from what is spoken to them. In the TEACCH modality, this issue is specifically addressed by visual supports and the expanding of existing skills by visual means. The use of visual supports has been found to be very helpful and is often used in combination with other methodologies. Events of a child's day can be illustrated with a visual schedule. This visual support system is a means of communicating the course of the day to the child simply and directly. Children with ASD benefit from knowing clearly what to expect in their day. Visual schedules can then be manipulated to help a child adapt to change. Use of visual supports is also helpful in breaking down organizational tasks into small visual components. This offers the child a step-by-step review of what needs to be accomplished in a way that does not involve verbal communication. Additionally, photos of friends help children learn to identify peers by name. The application of visual supports can be used in a variety of situations to support a child with ASD.

Emotion and relationship-based intervention methods

Yet another way to approach intervention for the child with ASD is to focus on the development of appropriate emotional response and relationship building. These programs prioritize the need to relate in "real-life" settings, and specific guidance is given on how to achieve that. A sample of one such program was designed by Greenspan (Greenspan and Wieder 1998). Stanley Greenspan, a psychiatrist from George Washington University, looks to relationship-based intervention rather than behavioral approaches. His approach is developmental because he sees PDD as a multisystem neurologic disorder (Greenspan and Wieder, p.8).

The Greenspan intervention method requires the manipulation of the child's environment to cultivate interrelation, engagement and sensory regulation. A primary emphasis of this model is on attaining more appropriate emotional responses. Listening and learning are not felt to be the way to reach children with ASD but rather developing real-life interactions, repeatedly, with the necessary guidance. Language is addressed first on the non-verbal level with promotion of gesturing. Affect is cued; in other words, children are trained how to emotionally respond. Work is done in small, manageable steps. Family involvement is also a cornerstone to this approach.

Another program, relationship development intervention (RDI), is a program designed by Drs Gutstein and Sheely (2002). This method seeks to promote emotional connections. These specialists consider the brain's growth to be a dynamic process that can be influenced by experience. The emphasis of the work is accomplished through interface and interaction. This model frames autism under concepts that are consistent with the core deficits of ASD but looks at them just a little bit differently to implement interventions. Social coordination, or the ability to regulate and modulate social behaviors is a targeted skill. Emotional referencing, declarative language, flexible thinking and relational information process, are all concepts that add appropriate breadth to the interventions. Parents are very active participants and interventions are broken down into steps and paced over time. Many programs and interventionists are utilizing some of the aspects of this method or modifying what this method has to offer.

Communication augmentation

Some programs emphasize the visual learning style of the child with ASD. Viewing the core deficit in ASD as that of an inability to understand the social communication process, these programs specifically implement certain visual strategies. One program that encompasses this idea with theory from the behavioral camp was designed by Andrew Bondy (Frost and Bondy 1994).

The picture exchange communication system (PECS) was developed to work specifically with children who have communication disorders that are due to a lack of social understanding and awareness. Behavioral techniques, such as giving a concrete reward, are combined with the use of pictures to foster communication. Children are initially prompted to make requests or initiate an exchange, and they do so with a tangible picture. The process is rewarded and success is then built upon. While this is not an extremely difficult procedure, it does require training in order to be most effectively implemented. The key concept of using visuals, and focusing on the need to develop social interaction, are components that can be applied to any teaching strategy for children with ASD.

Additional communication devises for non-verbal children are also available through assistive technology. Computer technology has been instrumental in further supporting children with special needs.

Implementing therapy

Now that you are a little familiar with the modalities being offered to children with ASD today, let's look at how one actually has the intervention implemented. We spoke briefly before about the issue of having interventions provided in the home, or in a more specialized school setting. If a parent has chosen to have the child receive servicing in the home environment, they are then in the position of finding the person, or people, to do that. Therapists and teachers who go into children's homes can either work independently, or work for a program, but visit the homes to provide servicing. In either case, a parent needs to select such a provider.

Selecting individual intervention specialists

Many therapists and special educators will meet with parents prior to being chosen as a provider. Others are unable to due to money and time constraints. If one cannot meet in person, perhaps they may be available by telephone interview. Some parents are intimidated by this process, but it is certainly their right to know something about a person prior to that person coming into their home to work with their child. Therapists often welcome an opportunity to address questions and issues ahead of time.

Ask the therapist or teacher what method she employs and why she uses that specific one. If she names a specific method, ask in what way she implements it. For example, if she uses ABA, does she do discrete trials or apply behavior modification in a play setting? If you are not familiar with the approach she uses, ask for more information about what they do in session with children. You may want to know how many years of experience the provider has and the extent of direct experience she has with children with ASD. The purpose of the questioning is to gather information and to then make a decision. If someone is new to the field you may not want to automatically disqualify her. She may just exude the energy and enthusiasm, or share one's philosophy to the extent that your gut (led by your head) tells you that this person can help your child.

Practical issues are a factor as well. When a therapist is available and how flexible he can be, may be an issue for a parent. Does this schedule work in the real everyday workings of a family?

How he sees the parent's role and how he intends to include the parent in intervention and decision-making is an important question. Most therapists have frequent, ongoing communication with the parents but, particularly if the parents work outside of the home and are unable to be at therapy sessions, this has to be firmly established ahead of time. Ideas to support good exchange are essential: a daily log for both therapist and parent to write in, a weekly phone conference, or even a monthly consultative meeting to discuss where the child is, gains they have made, needs that persist, and to evaluate the overall intervention plan and response.

Finally, if more than one therapist is going to be involved in a child's plan, parents will need to coordinate therapies. Parents need to get the sense that they will be team players and that the therapist is not a solo act.

Selecting a program

Many parents decide that their child would benefit most from the more intensive environment of a center-based program, or specialized school. After becoming familiar with the various general approaches, it is important for a parent to get out to see the programs in action. Seeing is believing, or, more correctly, seeing is understanding. A parent is then able to make an informed decision as to what program would be good for their child. Most programs will give prospective parents a tour, review pertinent issues and address questions. Often parents can observe therapy sessions. Viewing the techniques, settings and hands-on components demonstrates a lot to the informed viewer. Schools are generally receptive to parents, and if they aren't at this stage, perhaps that's an important piece of information in itself.

The first thing to address is a program's overall philosophy and intervention approach. What methods are used and who implements them? What sorts of therapists, teachers and specialists will be working with the child? What are their qualifications, experience and expertise? How much experience do they have in working with ASD and what sort of success have they noted with these children? Look at the actual structure and schedule of the day. How long is the day and what amount of time will the child be in individual sessions? How much time will he be in group activity? Is all the time spent in structured activity, or is there free time?

One parent shared with me that her child attended a program for four hours a day, only to find out that she was out of the classroom for three hours of it for individual therapy. The mother's main interest in this program was the social interaction afforded in a small group setting; however, the actual structure of the day prohibited the child from seeing much of her peers. They modified the program so the child received the private therapy sessions at her home in the afternoons and was able to be more a part of the group setting during her time at the school.

Some practical things come into play when choosing a program. What is the class size and the staff-to-child ratio? How much one-on-one time will your child have? What sorts of special needs do other participants have? One may not want a child with ASD in a setting in which none of the participants have verbal language or any communication skills, for example. It is perfectly reasonable to ask specifically how the program promotes social interaction. Establish what is done in more specific scenarios. For instance, if the child likes to spin when excited, how would the staff members deal with this? Or, a child talks incessantly about trains, how will the therapist alter that? How do they manage tantrums?

Be clear on the role of the parent as viewed by the school. How do parents fit into the scheme of things? What is the means and frequency of communication with parents? What is available for parent education and support?

Evaluation of progress is key to being able to make the necessary changes to an intervention plan. If a therapy technique is not working, it needs to be looked at, analyzed and revised. All programs should have a format for data keeping and evaluation. Evaluation should be planned and not just be sporadic. It is not good enough to just "sort of see where things are going." Ask the program providers directly how they plan to review the child's gains, assess his ongoing needs, and address those needs or make modifications over time.

Uniqueness of intervention and programming

After having reviewed these different educational modalities, and there are many more educational philosophies not addressed here, let us get back to the point at hand. There are many therapists and programs. Each utilizes different methods; teachers and therapists contribute their own unique gifts, and many incorporate a combination of therapy methods to optimize the child's development. Therefore, the punch line is not so much what modality a therapist or program espouses to use, but rather what they have to offer the individual child. You have probably ascertained that we, the authors, do not exclusively support any one modality. It has been our experience that different methods work for different children and combinations of strategies can be very beneficial. A consideration also has to be what a family can realistically employ day in and day out. Whatever method professionals, or program families go with, they need to be truly committed to participating in its success.

Some key points

Regardless of the specific method chosen:

1. Intervention plans need to specifically address communication and socialization skills.

2. Programming needs to be individualized and structured.

3. Professionals working with children with ASD should have appropriate background and experience.

4. The issue of generalization needs to be concretely addressed.

5. The program must record and review data over time. The evaluation of this information is then used to modify interventions as needed.

6. Parents need to be active participants involved in planning, implementing, and evaluating the child's programming.

7. The program should include a concrete means of regular communication and collaboration among teachers and therapists. Additionally, there should be a formulated means of communication with parents.

8. All professionals working with the child need to have a good understanding of the diagnosis of ASD and how the individual child presents with the disorder.

9. Health and safety requirements must be met.

Children with ASD in the school-age years

It is not uncommon for children on the mild end of the spectrum of ASD not to be diagnosed until they are school age. Also, children who were diagnosed with ASD at younger ages are being integrated into the typical classroom setting. The needs of many children with ASD are best served in a typical classroom, but almost always these children need additional support. The characteristics of ASD may present uniquely in the classroom setting and can easily be misunderstood. Behaviors perceived as socially odd may be misunderstood by peers and teachers. Other children may have a difficult time understanding unusual social approaches and literal comments may often be perceived as rude or offensive. A child with Asperger syndrome (AS), for example, may comment on a dirty shirt or tell another student that they broke a rule. Perseveration on specific topics, especially if they are not age-appropriate, does not go over big with peers. When a child talks incessantly about pokemon cards in sixth grade they may have a hard time building friendships in the classroom environment.

The child's inability to respond or participate may be misunderstood as defiance. Situations lead to the child being considered manipulative or having a behavior problem. Behavior problems often stem from misunderstood social overtures and poor communication abilities. Also, difficulties with emotional regulation and self-control play a large role in behavior management in the classroom. The child's inability to process the abundance of sensory information in various school environments also impact how that child is able to not only participate, but behave appropriately. The impairments in communication, socialization and restricted thinking, as well as the social and emotional pieces, are aspects of the developmental disorder and all who work with the child with ASD should have a clear understanding of this.

Learning problems may emerge in school-age children. Many children on the spectrum of autism have very strong skills in one area but may be totally lacking in another. The child who is doing tenth grade algebra in third grade can have the reading comprehension of a first grader. The complexity of the learning profiles of many children with ASD increase the challenges they face in the academic milieu of the school. It may be helpful to have a more clear understanding of a child's learning profile if needs arise or if a child is not moving forward academically. Specialists in psychoeducational testing can help sort out the nature of the child's learning style and offer a profile of strengths and weaknesses to help drive the educational programming and supports. Special supports should be designed for these children and they need to be very individualized. Special educators and subject tutors are often accessed to help lessen the gaps and promote better academic success.

Another issue to be addressed in regard to the child with ASD in the classroom has to do with their difficulties with rigidity and inflexibility. This can be helped markedly by keeping the classroom structured and predictable. The child with ASD should be prepared ahead of time for changes and transitions. The use of a timer to let him know when there are just a few minutes left to an activity can be a simple way to alleviate troubles involved in moving from one task to the other. Also, a sequence of events presented in pictures can be used as a tool to help a child with transition. They can be prompted, prior to a change in activity, to point or hand a picture to the teacher, a communication that they understand something else is going to happen.

For children with ASD, rigidity carries over to a fixation on concrete rules. These children can take rules very literally and will have a hard time following inconsistent use of rules. If they can't talk in line in the hallway, they may not understand why kids are talking in line in gym class. Rules need to be spelled out succinctly and followed as best as possible. Helping the child understand the flexibility in some rules can be achieved by training the concept. This is achieved by pointing out any time when they are flexible in a day by saying, "That was very flexible of you when you did XYZ." They then establish a more concrete understanding of the word and concept of flexible. When you later ask them to be flexible, they are able to follow the concept. This strategy can be applied to other concepts as well, such as: patience, understanding, attentiveness and cooperation.

Struggles with language can be managed in the classroom with the assistance of a speech therapist. Specific plans to assist the child with ASD in communicating his needs and wants should be a major focus of intervention in the classroom, as it was in the earlier years. Language used with the child should be concise and clear. A furrowing of the brow from across the classroom may not be enough to get Alex back in his chair. Again, utilization of schedules and pictorial representations of language can be very helpful tools.

The special interests of children with ASD can be used to advantage, by implementing them into the child's lessons. If a child loves trains, stickers with trains on them can be used as a manipulative in working through math problems. Special interests can also be used as rewards. For example, when Sam can sit and do his math for 10 minutes, he can then play with his train on the rug.

Problems with fine motor skills, or the child's ability to coordinate the use of his hands, may make it hard for children with ASD to work efficiently and in a timely fashion when handwriting is involved. The child shouldn't be pressured by time constraints whenever possible and accommodation for the additional time requirements should be taken into account. Occupational therapists can assist specifically in this area. It might be a reasonable consideration as a child gets older, to minimize the problem and stress of fine motor difficulties, by letting the child use a keyboard. When writing by hand is inhibiting the ability to get one's thoughts and information expressed, then perhaps it is appropriate to take that issue out of the equation of struggles.

Early reading skills are sometimes an area of strength for children with ASD. Though they can often read well mechanically, their comprehension may be behind. For this reason, they seem to have advanced reading abilities, while in fact they actually need remediation. Getting the content of what has been read, and picking up on emotional components of what they have read, may need to be more directly taught. There are so many wonderful books available to children, with a content that can foster better social understanding and provide a situation for the teacher to discuss social circumstances. This provides an avenue for the teacher to expand on the child's social understanding. Early reading can be capitalized on, but may need to be expanded upon by specialized help.

Children with ASD are not immune to the impact of others. As a matter of fact, older children with AS have taught us that the reverse can be true. They are acutely aware of their differences and make a great deal of effort to be socially accepted. This is a hard task for many children. They may feel lonely and isolated, and this can lead to low self-esteem. They have to conscientiously work on issues that their peers pick up instinctively. This is a constant challenge for them. Attention needs to be paid to this issue and teachers, parents, and all who work with children with ASD, need to help build up, rather than break down these children. Positive reinforcement and praise goes a lot further than discipline and denigration. If symptoms of emotional problems arise, they should be addressed promptly with the assistance of professionals.

The child's development is not just about his special needs. Like for all children, parents should be involved in school activities. This indicates an interest in the child's world. Friendships can be fostered by getting children together or encouraging the child with ASD to join groups that share his interests. It can be hard for some children with ASD to play one-on-one initially, so it may be helpful to set up play dates by going to a museum or some other activity that incorporates social interaction but is not totally reliant on it. Praise social successes with the vigor one would applaud athletic or academic success.

Additional tips

Communication assistance

Various communication tools that don't involve speech have been tried for children who have significant difficulties with language. Communication boards, or picture boards, are used to promote communicative exchange while not requiring the child to speak. Usually the boards have pictures of desired objects or actions and the child communicates by getting the picture off the board. There are some very elaborate computer communication boards available today. However, before incurring the expense of these, know what it is that you are buying. Look to people familiar with this assistive device technology for further advisement.

A lot can be done more simply. One therapist shared with me the type of board she finds useful. She begins by taking photographs of things the child likes. She initially keeps them in the 8 x 10 inch size and the child actually chooses the whole picture under certain prompts or questions. When the child demonstrates a good understanding of what the pictures represent, the therapist shrinks the picture to a smaller size. She continues to do this until they are small and can go on a Velcro board. The child continues to actually pick the picture off the board to communicate. Eventually, this progresses to pointing at the picture on the board. In this whole process, verbal and non-verbal language reinforces the visual.

Use of computers

Computers are powerful tools to children with ASD. For one thing, many children with ASD respond well to the concrete nature of a computer's functions. What you exactly tell a computer to do, it does. There is no need for much language interpretation with a computer. Children with ASD may have capabilities on the computer and these can be used to expand into other areas. It is not helpful to the child with ASD to sit down to do something rote and repetitive on the keyboard while tuning out the world around them. The use of the computer needs to be supervised to be beneficial. There are programs available of children's stories which are interactive and will promote interaction and expansion on social understanding. There are also programs designed specifically for special needs children that focus on language and communication. Communication skills training, language, activities of daily living, and many other topics are addressed by the multitudes of specialized interactive programs currently available. There are many specifically geared toward the development of conversational abilities and social understanding, not strictly language acquisition.

One final word

Education is a lifelong process. It is important to offer appropriate interventions and educational opportunities throughout life. It is also important to keep in perspective that the education process is only part of the life process. Naturalized learning in family rooms, neighborhood gatherings, church basements, and playgrounds offer important lessons not set up by any therapist or teacher. We encourage parents to embrace the life experiences that childhood offers to the benefit of the whole family.

Additional Options

Alternative therapies

Alternative therapies are essentially treatments that are somewhat outside of mainstream, or may not have been adequately studied for their effects or side-effects. There is significant confusion as to the role of medical approaches to autistim spectrum disorders (ASD). Some experts would say that there is NO definitive medical approach and that all interventions should be behavioral and educational. Other experts would say that there are a whole variety of approaches that could be tried in generally what are call biomedical areas. While there are plenty of internet sites claiming their approach is the best way, for example, true objective information is often hard to come by. Should your child have a special diet, take supplements, use oxygen, be detoxified by various means or have his or her immune "boosted"? There is so much information available and much of it promotes a particular perspective. What would be helpful then would be to have some way of sorting through the multitude of these claims.

Parents and professionals have tried a wide variety of treatments and interventions that were found to be helpful to a child, or a group of children. What works well for one, however, may do nothing for another. Parents have always searched for the one thing that will make a difference to their child. This is a good thing as parents are a powerful driving force behind the research work that is being done currently. A problem can arise, however, when information is shared on something that worked for one individual child and is then applied to all children without adequate study.

Testimonials, or the accounts of singular cases, can be helpful in a parent's attempts to share with others what has worked for their child; however, these should be viewed with some caution. A certain treatment may work for one but this does not mean that it is necessarily good for every child to try, or that it might not be harmful to a different child. The intention of this chapter is not to discourage parents from trying natural treatments or from sharing non-conventional treatments with others if they so desire. It is our hope that parents will be informed on how to better evaluate treatments, the validity of their use, and be able to identify potentially harmful treatments.

"Natural"

Be aware that just because a substance is deemed natural it does not mean that it is automatically harmless. Let us remember that some very strong drugs were derived from perfectly natural plants. Digoxin, a heart medication, comes from a foxglove plant for instance. Taken by the wrong person, it could have potentially serious deleterious effects. One can look at hormones as natural substances, but be reminded that they have some very powerful effects in the body. Think of insulin, the hormone responsible for controlling blood sugar levels. If it were given to a child with normal blood sugar levels it could be very harmful, if not lethal. Some naturally occurring substances need to be at a particular level in the body. Health food stores are very much in vogue these days for curing an array of ailments. People tend to be moving toward what they perceive to be more natural and harmless substances. This is not necessarily untrue, but one needs to be an informed consumer. So how does one become an informed consumer in the light of the contradictory evidence that is out there regarding just about everything?

Here are some suggestions of questions to ask:

1. Physical and emotional harm issues need to come first. Is the treatment safe? And, how do we know it is safe?

2. Is the treatment effective?

To answer these first two questions we need to look to the information regarding the claim. Is there some independent, well-evaluated information available as to its safety and effectiveness? It is not enough for a provider to support that a treatment may have a positive effect; there should be some outside confirmation of this. Claims of safety and effectiveness based on testimony of others are really not enough. Are there studies done under scientific methods that are the standard of our evaluation of treatments for children (controlled, blinded studies) that are available to the consumer?

3. Does the information have good basis in physiology, neurology and biology? Explanations sometimes sound fancy and scientific but actually have a very poor connection to good science.

4. Is there someone who can monitor the treatment who is independent of the treatment provider and offer an outside judgment as to response?

5. Is there a financial gain for those providing the intervention? There are people making money from unproven interventions. It only makes it worse that well-intentioned parents are believing in them.

Looking at treatments

First consider the testing and regulation of a given product. Most non-drug products are not regulated under the guidelines of the Food and Drug Administration (FDA). The FDA has very strict policies for the testing and administration of medications, and rightly so. It does not, however, have control over vitamin and mineral treatments, or even some of the more recent hormonal compounds. This means that there is no oversight, and no consistency among brands, regarding scientific testing of a substance. These substances often lack the testing that rationally and impartially questions product usefulness and safety.

Does this product have possible side-effects? What is appropriate dosing? How is it prepared in a compound for administration and what is it combined with to make it have a stable shelf life? Recently, a compound felt to stimulate memory had to be pulled off the shelf because it was prepared in an alcohol compound and under-age children were taking it for the alcohol component, not to do better in their social studies exams. All this does not mean that one should never take a vitamin. It is just intended to encourage a parent to put up an antenna and find out as much as possible about something that their child is going to ingest, before making the decision to give it to them.

When looking at non-conventional treatments, there are options other than diets, vitamins, minerals and hormones. When considering the safety of these methods, it is not as critical as the child may be spending time on something that isn't fully "proven," yet they are not ingesting something that may be harmful. Therapies such as holding therapy, or dance and movement therapy, don't pose any physical harm and may help some children. Horseback riding, swimming with dolphins, and various animal programs are now available in most areas. Parent should still look objectively at how the child, and they, are spending their time. Time and energy is a valuable entity when raising children.

There is a tremendous maze of claims for helpful or curative approaches to ASD. However, claims that are not well-studied and open to impartial review must always be looked at carefully. When in doubt, a parent is wise to call a medical center or a trusted medical professional to help with the overwhelming preponderance of information on multiple alternative therapies.

An alarming example of a claimed cure

A good example of a previous popular intervention was the use of the hormone secretin. There were very strong testimonials as to how well it worked, how safe it was. This naturally occurring hormone was given a very favorable slant by media coverage in the United States. Anecdotal reports of children with autism whose symptoms decreased after receiving secretin were the subject of several television reports. These reports stimulated many parents to ask about the treatment and seek administration of it for their children. While it is quite reasonable to have a positive initial response to such information, it is important to slow down and examine the information more closely.

Secretin is essentially a substance secreted by the pancreas that assists in the process of neutralizing stomach acids. It is used currently in the medical community during diagnostic testing of the intestinal tract. Some information publicized through television media showed children with ASD given secretin were observed to have improved communication and social skills. The findings were quite promising but were limited. The excitement proceeded evaluation of the substance and its effectiveness, later changing the excitement to disappointment. Further research demonstrated no convincing improvement noted in children with ASD when given the hormone. Additionally, significant concerns were raised regarding short and long-term side effects. The media coverage died down and so did the use of this unproven treatment.

Many important scientific discoveries stem from random occurrences and clinical observations. The next step still needs to be taken, careful evaluation of a presumed treatment. Controlled research provides the accurate answers we seek and it is to this we must look. Parents and professionals in the field of developmental pediatrics are very committed to supporting such research. It is an optimistic future.

The quest for information

The net

In this day and age we would be remiss if we didn't address the internet and the volume of information literally at the finger tips of parents and professionals. There is something for everyone on the net and surfing it can prove to be beneficial, and overwhelming. The need to weed out what is valid and what is useless can be an arduous process. It can be worthwhile for those seeking to tap into resources and to connect with other parents and professionals out of their area. Parents need to remember that the World Wide Web is a place for everyone. Anyone can put up any kind of information they wish. Well-meaning people and those out for material gain may publish approaches or information that is misleading, misguided, or inappropriate. When you see information, be certain that the source is reliable. The source should have some tie to a university, medical school, reputable agency, or well-established and respected private program. Look at claims and treatments closely. Are there data to support the claim? Has valid research been accomplished?

Support groups

Support groups can be very helpful to parents. There is nothing like working through problems with someone who has been there. Parents are cautioned that in some of these groups, however, there is the natural desire to compile children into the same expectations. Parents of children with ASD need to be particularly aware of the uniqueness of their children and use such groups which support and embrace those differences. Support groups can be cathartic, help parents make connections to other families, give a forum for concerns, and be a place for advocacy to begin.

To summarize

Before starting any intervention, the family and treatment team should

- identify the target problem they are addressing

- develop a reliable system to track potential change over time

- implement interventions by one change at a time in a stepwise fashion so as to be sure which step is most effective.

Take caution; be an educated consumer

- cautiously look at claims of CURE

- cautiously look at information about the successfulness of an intervention based on testimonials

- seek scientific review and referenced supports

- cautiously view interventions that are financially costly.

Up Close and Personal: Parents and Young People Share their Stories

The inspiration for the original edition of this book and this revision was spawned from the desire to support families and children with autistim spectrum disorder (ASD). Following the release of the first edition, parents shared with us that they enjoyed the stories and could relate to the issues that were addressed. These interviews touched us the first time around and in the process of revisiting this book, new interviews have been added. You will notice that we spoke to Bobby's parents several years ago and they were able to join us again. Additionally, two teens on the autistic spectrum shared their stories and gave a tremendous view of their experience and perspective. New interviews speak to the multitude of educational interventions available and the ability to learn about them more readily. There is indeed much insight to be gained from the sharing of these stories.

Please note that the names of the children and the parents have been changed to protect confidentiality. While much of the interview contents are verbatim from the participants, some have been abridged and/or modified in an attempt to be more concise and understandable. The main ideas are those of the participants.

A special thank you to those who shared so openly. It is their desire, as it is ours, that other parents will learn and be comforted by what they have to say. Here are their stories.

Bobby

Bobby's story is unlike the others in that his parents were not surprised by the diagnosis of Asperger syndrome but rather were relieved. They had intuitively sensed that something was different about their child and had done quite a bit of research to better understand those differences. The research, and input of others, led them to the diagnosis of Asperger syndrome before they "officially" received that label. The process was not an easy one, however, and Bobby's early years were tumultuous times for his family. Bobby's father, Rob, shares his frustrations, challenges, and triumphs in their story.

Early years

Bobby was a very good baby right from the beginning. He was a great eater and a great sleeper. At two months the doctor recommended that we drop his night-time bottle. The next night we didn't go in when he woke in the middle of the night, and we never had to again. At around six months of age he started with ear infections. He had a lot of them and cried a lot. For a while we told ourselves that he had become fussy because of the ear infections. But, we had a feeling, especially Judy, my wife, that something was wrong early on. We didn't talk about it a whole lot back then. We might have said, "Boy, that seems like something other than an ear infection." But we didn't really talk about it a lot. We were willing to rationalize his differences at that point.

I can remember times when we went out places or to family member's house and I was the only one he would let hold him. He wouldn't even let anyone touch him, not even his hands. We thought, "Oh wow, maybe his ears hurt so much that everything hurts."

Concerns worsen

Between a year-and-a-half to two-and-a-half we noticed that he was having problems. If we went to someone's house, even a small crowd, he would instantly have problems. When he became mobile, which he did around one, he wouldn't go off with other kids. He's got several cousins and we would get together and he wouldn't interact with the other kids. All the other kids would be off playing. Bobby would cling to me or tantrum. That started to bother us. I wasn't too worried at that point because when we were home he was happy; he seemed okay. He had a large book collection and he would flip through the books by himself. He didn't need someone reading them to him. You could put him next to a pile of books and return in an hour to find the books stacked on the other side of him. He would have looked through each one and he wouldn't have moved. He was happy with it so we didn't make a big deal of it. But, then we got to the point that we would try to push him to go play with the other kids so we could have some time with adults, and he would resist us. Sometimes he would go, but then he would call us in a very short time to come about a little thing that shouldn't have bothered him.

He started talking right on time. If you want specific details you have to talk to my wife. She will know the date, time, and place exactly. As I recall, even around a year he was actually pointing at a tree and saying, "tee". He was gesturing and seemed to understand communication. He would do stuff for us at home where he was comfortable that he wouldn't do anywhere else, though. He talked mostly to us.

At home, things were not so out of sorts. Judy was really tuned in though. She sensed something was going on early. I was sort of chalking it up to, "Hey, he's just being shy" or, "He's just quiet." Judy picked up that it wasn't normal. I have to admit that I was frustrated. On a selfish front I was maybe even embarrassed at times. I thought, "Why isn't our kid like the rest of the kids?" I wondered if other parents were thinking, "How are they raising this kid?" When Bobby was content with something, I would stop worrying. It started to bother me more when I felt that Bobby was upset about it too. It was like he wanted to be in there with other kids but he wasn't letting himself go.

Response to wife's concerns

Judy was around Bobby a whole lot more than I was. She had a lot more exposure to him. So, even though I wasn't all that concerned initially, I figured that there had to be something to what she was concerned about. I didn't really communicate that to her so much, it was more to myself. At that point, when she really started to have serious concerns, it was difficult for her to just get through the day and I didn't want to add to those concerns. He had started to be easily upset by minor changes in his routine. It made for a tough day for mom at home with her first child. We spent a lot more time just trying to get through the hours rather than spending much time sitting around talking about it. It was the end of the day when I came home from work and we would just hope that the next day would be better for him.

Judy was able to get into a routine with Bobby that made things manageable. He really did well when things were kept the same. Some days when I literally walked in the door I would throw everything off. It would cause the day to swing out of control. I think there was a breaking of the routine. Judy would have a nice equilibrium going, and I would walk in the door and shatter that. Just by walking in the door! Because we only had a couple hours in the evening every day, my routine wasn't to come home like a typical guy and say, "I'm gonna go home and play with my kid." He didn't seem to feel comfortable when I came in. That was hard. I was frustrated that I didn't have much time with him. I was frustrated because I knew that Judy's day was hard, and I was making things worse. I was frustrated that I couldn't relate to my son. I was frustrated because I didn't know why I made things worse. It was all very frustrating and difficult to accept. Selfishly, personally, I felt bad for myself, but I felt bad for them too. I felt part of the problem. I felt helpless not knowing what I could do differently. Should I be more strict, or less strict? I was trying everything, knowing nothing.

Diagnosed Asperger syndrome

Around two-and-a-half Bobby really cut loose at the doctor's office so she finally agreed, for the first time, that something might not be quite right. He tantrummed so bad and was so out of control that she thought maybe there was something to our concerns. She really didn't have any major suspicion but she wanted to rule out anything that might have been major. She thought that maybe he was having seizures so she referred us to a neurologist. The neurologist couldn't really do anything because Bobby was so upset at the first visit that the doctor couldn't even examine him. This was a hard time. When I went to the visits it seemed to make Bobby worse. I wanted to be there, but I knew it was harder for everyone because I was there. Again, I felt like part of the problem and not able to help my own son, and wife. The neurology visit was so bad that we could hardly even talk to the doctor. After that Judy took him to the visits alone. I felt like a bystander, for my own son. I was out of the mix.

At just over two years old, we took Bobby to see a psychologist who essentially told us it was about our parenting. Apparently, he felt we needed to be better disciplinarians. That wasn't particularly helpful.

After that, Judy took Bobby to another neurologist. I wasn't at this meeting because we knew it would throw Bobby off. That was hard, to know something was up and that my wife had to go alone. At the same time, we knew it was the right decision. The neurologist was particularly interested in Bobby's symptoms. She was actually enthralled with what she saw. In hindsight, despite the frustrations, difficulties and all that, you could see what a special little kid he was. He was incredibly intelligent, creative, and had a sense of humor, even from a very young age. I think the neurologist saw him as a mix of his strengths and weaknesses. Bobby was a fascinating child. The neurologist threw out the term Asperger's, but didn't know too much about it at that point so she referred us to a developmental pediatrician. We both did a lot of reading before that visit and we became pretty confident that Bobby fit that diagnosis. After we read about the disorder, we definitely saw some of the symptoms of Asperger's but we saw these other things too.

It was given a name

After it was given the name, Asperger syndrome, we started the research around here. We read everything that we could get our hands on. We would have been surprised if it hadn't been called Asperger's by the time we went to the developmental pediatrician because we had read so much that sounded like Bobby. The idea that it was something that somebody knows about was a relief. Okay, he's not a brat. We're not doing something wrong here as parents. We had gotten many different pieces of advice and people had suggested that it was about our parenting. We felt pretty sure that wasn't the case because we had started seeing problems at such an early age. He had trouble being comforted, or comforting himself as an infant. He had trouble with rigidity of routine as an infant. At some level, we knew it wasn't about us. But, there was a relief in the confirmation of that and in it having a name. We didn't know much about it, but we knew it was something with a name.

There was sadness too. The idea that maybe he was just a difficult toddler, and he's just going to out grow this was gone. And, the uncertainty of, "What does this really mean?" was unsettling. There were some fears. Overall, I thought, "Okay, there's something wrong, and there are people out there that we can work with." I think that up until then we had been floundering. Trying one thing that would seem to work for a while, then all of a sudden it would stop working. We would try something else. He would take to almost anything we would try, for a brief time. After the diagnosis we were able to focus our efforts.

Starting services

After that we went to quite a few places that service children with special needs. They were all different. Some of them actually struck terror in my heart. To see all the levels of disability and to have a child in this arena was very scary. Some classrooms seemed too extreme for Bobby. I don't think that it was denial on our parts. We said, "Okay, he's got this but it's not at the extreme end of the spectrum. It is a part of him but it is not all of him." We wanted to get him help but we wanted him to get the right kind of help. He was very impressionable. He was a very good mirror. We felt that if he were exposed to severe behavioral disabilities he would mimic those behaviors.

Eventually, we did find a program that we liked very much. There were special needs kids of different levels but it also seemed pretty typical. And, Bobby seemed to immediately fit in there.

Fixations

One of the things about Bobby is that while we know he has Asperger's we also see things about him that don't exactly fit with what we read. Yes, he has fixations but they change over time. They don't stay the same. They last about two to three months and then he gets a new obsession. The first one I remember was when he was just beginning to talk. I taught him the names of the Dwarfs and I could just see his little mind memorizing them. He would say, "Who dat?" And, quickly he knew them all and recited them regularly and in different orders. Then it became trucks, then dinosaurs, that was a big one. Now it seems to be Pokemon. He knows way beyond what you would think a kid would know about these things.

I noticed very early that he really enjoys numbers. He loves to count. He got off the school bus the other day and said that he had counted to 500 on the way home. I asked him, "Five-hundred what?" And he said, "Just five-hundred numbers." I think it calms him, like whistling or singing would. He does seem to have exceptional skills with numbers. In kindergarten he is doing addition and subtraction. Numbers have been an interest that has persisted throughout all the others. Number concepts are just something that he has always felt really comfortable with. He also loves puzzles. He would do the wooden ones over and over as a little guy. He still can occupy himself for a long time with puzzles.

His social world

Bobby saw his cousins a fair amount and, even though he was comfortable with them, he really wouldn't socialize in a group. He just seemed to have no interest in other kids. School really helped in this area. I could tell from day one at the school that he was going to do better there. At first he held back a little bit but then the teacher came over and he went with her. He went without even much coaxing. I don't know if it was that it was so much of an unfamiliar situation that he just didn't know to be nervous or what. He seemed to join right in. Judy and I watched from the sidelines amazed.

There were all kinds of toys around the classroom and he went to take something off the shelf. The teacher said, "No, Bobby come play with these." She directed him to put the toys back and then to join the others with the toys on the floor. Judy grabbed my hand and had tears in her eyes. We thought that he was going to cut loose, but he just went with it. That was when the light bulb went off and we knew that the schooling was going to give him something that we couldn't give him. The teacher was so matter of fact in directing him and she knew how to handle him. He settled right into the programming and we almost immediately saw him start to change socially. Right away he wanted to know the names of the other kids in his class and he learned them.

Kindergarten

After the positive preschool programming we decided to put him in regular kindergarten. The only special servicing that he started with there was speech therapy. That was mostly for articulation problems. We also had a monthly consultation with psychology just to keep on top of things. We didn't have direct servicing for Bobby, but we didn't want to pull the rug out from under him either. We didn't want to hide the diagnosis. We know that it can manifest itself in different ways at different times, so we are always on the look out. We want the school to be too, so we didn't want to hide anything from them. He is doing better than we hoped to be mainstreamed with no supports in the regular classroom. The teacher has the diagnosis in the back of her mind but she tells us that he is a delight to have in class. We knew he had come a long way but we were surprised to have him go into regular kindergarten with such little support.

Family and friends' reaction to Asperger's

I think that before the diagnosis people did think that he was different because of the way we were raising him. After the diagnosis was official everyone (family and friends) came right on board and were very supportive. Until that point I think, in part, that the family might have been in denial and, in part, they thought that we should just "straighten him out." Since the diagnosis though, they have all been totally supportive. It has made a big difference.

The future

When I look to the future I am very hopeful. There is concern still. He is only five and as he grows his friends also grow so the social challenges will continue. He is probably never going to be totally free of the Asperger symptoms. We still see a real struggle with the empathy issue. He just can not see another's point of view or feelings. In his day-to-day interactions things have to go by his own rules. That is not always going to work in the world and that concerns me. Other kids won't understand that perspective and I'm afraid that he won't fit in. I'm also afraid that he will be ostracized.

Role as father and husband

I don't know so much about the specifics of the dates and times of how all this transpired. Judy knows all the particulars. I didn't feel so much that I was pushed out of the picture. It was more that I felt helpless when I was in the picture. I was more than helpless; I made things worse for my son and wife. I disrupted the routine that was so important to Bobby feeling secure. I felt I let them down in some ways, but it wasn't a matter of choice. I did selfishly feel I was playing a different role than most fathers get to play.

The other thing that was hard was to feel like I had to justify Bobby's behaviors. If a child has a disability that you can see, say he is in a wheelchair or blind, no one would question the child's behaviors. When children look like other kids but act differently it's hard to explain. There were times I felt I had to justify Bobby's actions. I did feel worse for him, though, than for myself.

Whether having a child with Asperger's makes you stronger or weaker as a couple has to do with what you do with it. At first, Bobby's struggles consumed us. It literally became our life. We tried to keep some of ourselves alive but we weren't very successful at it. It wasn't until we got the diagnosis and started getting the support of the school that we were able to see how consumed we were with Bobby's needs. Once things started to get better for him we realized we needed to live life a little ourselves, and with each other as a couple. If we hadn't realized this, and turned things around, it could have been very destructive.

I have to add that going through this situation with Judy has showed me a lot about her. She was the reason we identified this so early and got him help at such a young age. The strains this may have caused built into a sincere, incredible appreciation of my wife. She has shown me strength that I find amazing!

"Life has treated me well"

I admit that there have been frustrating and embarrassing times as a parent, but I have to say that I am incredibly proud of my son. He is not just along for the ride. He is clearly part of the solution. He has put in so much effort and he has made such progress. I remember watching him when he wasn't even three years old and he knew that he had done something wrong. It was as if he was watching himself from outside of himself. My pride for him outweighs any possible embarrassment.

I have had a lot go my way in life. Life has treated me well. This really is one of the first challenges to my faith. It definitely has its negative side, but so much of our life is still "silver-lined." Even with Asperger syndrome, Bobby is such a special guy. We always saw him that way. There are so many positives and I have a lot of faith in him.

Bobby: the story told years later

We first met Bobby in the original edition of this book. He was just a young boy then and we returned to talk to his mother about his life since we last spoke. A strong, handsome young man answered the door and greeted me with a smile. While the young man's eyes were reminiscent of the little boy I once met, his demeanor had changed. His animated smile turned to an inquisitive gaze as he greeted me. Later his mother told me she had just recently showed him our first interview. Bobby has done remarkably well and is now looking at colleges. While he was not part of this discussion with his mother, he offered his eighth grade speech which is at the end of this section. It speaks for itself.

His mother once again generously shares with great pride and sense of humor. The crystal ball she once sought has the childhood section illuminated and behind her. We walk through that crystal ball as she tells their story.

What is your response to reading the story first published?

It takes me back, boy. When I pulled out the box where I keep the book, there is a lot of other information. Journals I wrote back and forth with the teachers that had a lot of the things that we struggled with at the time. That was hard to read again. It's like labor I guess. You remember it as not so bad at the time. I often say, I wouldn't change a thing. And I think that trivializes it because having read that again, I realize I wouldn't want to go through some of that again. When I did read the book again, though, I found the same sense of relief as when people started working with us. The feeling of, "There, someone gets it". Someone understands this and knows more about it than I do. It became a happy experience reading the story. Actually, it was a happy story even when we were still in it. That's not just because he came out the other side. I remember feeling good that people knew something about what we were dealing with. Giving Bobby's struggles a name, not only the name, but the notion that there was something we could do to help him, was a such a good thing.

In our first interview you wished you had a crystal ball.

I was just talking to Bobby about this today. Two things stick out to me. One was the notion that I wished I had a crystal ball that would show me that life was tolerable. When he was first diagnosed he was in the throws of the tantrums, unable to wear certain clothes, not able to play with other kids and life was just not good for him back then. All I could do was transfer that to when he was older and think that life was not going to be good for him. As soon as we had a diagnosis, I thought there would be a treatment and I wanted to see in the crystal ball what he looked like at the end of that treatment. Little did I know how far he would exceed any expectation I had. Life is not just tolerable. Life is fantastic for him!

And, for you?

I want to help other parents and children in small ways. I'm on Facebook; I've met people in early intervention programs, and chat rooms. I try to encourage parents who have any questions about their child to seek help. One of the groups is called, "When in doubt, seek services out." I also tell parents, I wouldn't change it. I wouldn't change a thing about him. Even now, on some days when he's rigid or not responding emotionally right I think of it more as his personality. But I look back on all the documentation of the early days and I remember how hard it is to be in the middle of it. I try to share that with other parents and help them look forward.

At what point did it shift from being a developmental disorder to how you see it now as a personality type?

When I stopped having to fix Bobby's day and he started to actually resist my help. When I was able to back away from that I realized that he was figuring out his own coping strategies. I needed to say to myself, "Okay, maybe he's not going to want play dates." He wasn't drawn to meeting other kids but he wasn't unhappy. He was comfortable with neighborhood kids and he would hang out with them. I had to adjust what I thought should be making Bobby happy and what was really making Bobby happy. I had to realize that he may not show that he is happy by doing back flips through the house and I was a back flip through the house kind of person. Just because he wasn't smiling and laughing didn't mean he wasn't happy.

He started Tai Kwon Do in the first grade and that was huge for him. It was a non-team sport. It wasn't competitive and it was all about him. If he came home and practiced he got rewarded for that. He was good at memorizing the exact movements and forms he was to make. We sat back, watched and over a few years we just saw that things were getting better for him. We started to take a break in running the show, his show. Was he successful 100 percent of the time, no, he still had his issues. He would be perceived as rude because he would say something that was brutally honest and you found yourself explaining things to people. But I did become aware that I didn't need to make excuses for him. He was no more out there than many other people.

Tell me about what moved him in such a good direction.

He was first diagnosed at three-and-a-half, and he went to a special needs preschool program that focused on children with pervasive developmental disorders. He had special education, occupational therapy and speech. Even though he had really incredible language he was very stilted in his speech and gave a lot of inappropriate responses. We also had an individual specialist work on his play skills. We wanted him to have more imaginative play. He made a lot of progress, he seemed more connected and we thought he was doing great. So we went to see another doctor to get some sort of stamp of approval to send him into regular school. Well that doctor thought he needed all kinds of support and wouldn't make it in a regular classroom. My initial thought was, "You don't know him." Here I was ready to take any advice he had to give if he said Bobby was doing good, but now I wasn't going to take any advice.

We stepped away from it for a while and then we just decided to go with our guts. We met with a teacher from a private school and talked about things. She was very welcoming and was getting a Master's in special education. She was calm and patient and had a good understanding of what we were concerned about. So from there we went to the orientation and registration. I held my breath because they were taking the kids off somewhere. I thought, "Here we go…" The teacher took his hand, he never looked back and I knew we needed to try it. We needed to take a leap of faith and we decided to go with it. We put him in the regular classroom in what we thought was a somewhat protected environment. I look back and think maybe we were shielding him from the public system, services and all.

I think our gut was right and things were in alignment for him. We'd hear words like "quirky" to describe him, but you also heard that he was a riot. His second grade teacher was a very even-keeled teacher and she brought out the best in him. She told me he corrected her all the time and it drove her crazy. But she certainly appreciated him for who he was.

Tell me more about following your gut?

This is hard because I am so much for any type of service. It is not invasive, no one's doing surgery on these kids. His preschool had typically developing children and the program benefited them too. So, it's hard to explain how I made some of my decisions. In the end I just knew when we were able to move forward. I don't think you can take things at face value. You have to look at what it means to your child. When the school district told us that Bobby needed a full-time shadow aide what that really meant was that an adult would be following Bobby around and prompting him to respond to situations. What we had found was that he was able to respond appropriately 90 percent of the time, so we felt that a 100 percent shadowing was going to actually stop him from coming up with spontaneous responses on his own. We wanted him to come up with responses on his own and learn that it was okay. We also trusted that other kids would call him on wrong or unusual responses.

How did things progress?

We got him into the private school and kindergarten was wonderful. We had been told early on about the things children like Bobby never do. What they won't be able to achieve in their lives. I remember hearing that toilet training might be very difficult and kindergarten might not be a possibility. I took that as a challenge. These became the things I was going to make sure he did. But then we talked to some other people who really understood autistic spectrum disorders and someone told us that some of the things that are so limiting now may be applauded later, like his neatness and perseverance. Now maybe he can't stand one eraser mark on a paper and he's stuck on a certain juice cup, but later he'll stick with something that other people wouldn't be able to. I thought, "Okay, that's where we're going to go with this." We tried to take some of these idiosyncrasies and start to define them as positive attributes. The school came on board with that too. I have things he drew in kindergarten that look like an artist did them. I started to see people appreciate who Bobby was. These teachers saw that they had this kid in their class who was bright, eager to learn and had a very dry sense of humor. I used to tell them that it was a riot as long as you weren't living with it 24/7. I think we began to see that Bobby was figuring out life and teachers began to figure out how to respond to him. I found teachers eager and willing to get to really know Bobby.

Jumping forward in eighth grade Bobby gave a speech. It was quite humorous and he addressed every teacher in a very comical yet respectful way. People were laughing. Then he said, "They say that you learn everything you need to know in kindergarten." His kindergarten teacher was there. He said, "She taught me that not only was it okay to want my crayons lined up, but that hers were too."

Tell me about the school more.

It is a private Christian school. The class sizes are large, up to 25 children. He went from kindergarten to eighth grade in this school. I don't want to say we were without stumbling blocks.

The first day was a big stumbling block. We panicked to see so much of his negative behaviors come back. We had some dishevelment at home with family staying with us and it was just too much. He became very rigid, checking his backpack at night over and over. He'd say, "I forgot something", over and over. I was ready to not look back at that point and then all this stuff was there again.

In first grade I remember that he had a lot of stress. In journal writing at school he was so literal he couldn't complete the entries. For example, the question was, "What is the one thing you will never forget?" He wrote an answer and erased it and did that over and over. He got very irritated. Finally he was able to say to us, "How will I know what I will never forget?" Eventually he wrote his name. We realized why he was struggling so with the entries and why they were causing such havoc. He was taking them too literally. It did get better and he worked through a lot of that. But that was a rough year for him.

In second grade, he had another great teacher and he seemed to really make strides again. He just settled in.

Did you request specific teachers for him over the years?

Laughter. I tried that early on and learned my lesson. I had first wanted this perfect preschool teacher, this heavy set older woman with a big smile. Well, the classroom teacher was replaced and this woman came out with camouflage shorts, red nail polish and spiky hair. I was completely set back. I watched as she wiped Bobby's face and he started to stress about something. And, she just said, "Come on" and took him off. I literally got sick on the way home. I panicked because this was not what we had signed up for. I started to calm down and my husband said, "Why don't we see what Bobby thinks?" Bobby said, "I get to go back there tomorrow?" all excited. All right I thought, we'll try it but it's not going to work. Then I went to pick him up and I saw him walking across the lawn holding the teacher's hand and kicking at the tall grass. I just watched him, happy and following along. I thought, "Reality check, you just need to step back." I asked for the help, here was the help, now I needed to take the help.

I thought I learned my lesson but then I did request a teacher later on because she was so organized and had such strict routines. Again, not so good a year. I think that time I really learned my lesson. I found that when the school assigned him to a teacher that they had their reasons and usually those teachers were very invested in Bobby. Never again did I request a teacher. With each year, the teacher built on what he had achieved the prior year. I was able to really step back. Early on I would write a letter to the teacher telling them what he was going to need, and then I just stopped all that. He was making his own way. We stopped hearing all the things that were wrong, and started hearing the things that were right.

How did he do as he got up to fifth grade?

He started to get rambunctious. I remember saying to myself, "Be careful what you wish for." I had always wanted him to come out of his shell and here he was. I found myself explaining his whole story to his teacher, and she said, "Quite honestly, they're all like that at this age." You forget that some stuff is normal development, like adolescence. The second he would cut up or something we would wait for the other shoe to drop. But it didn't. We are constantly reminded that this is life. It's not perfect and it can be messy. It's hard when you go from helping to control their entire environment and then you have to let them make mistakes. I reminded myself that I hadn't wanted a shadow aide so why was I going to try to do that myself. I had to trust that if he made social mistakes the kids around him would pull him into line. He had to get his own tools. I remember him telling me when he was just little that he had a stop button on his belly and if he pushed on it the stress would stop. I would see him pushing his button from time to time. Ultimately, they do need to have their own buttons I guess.

Junior high went surprisingly well. He really started to learn from the other kids. His grades were great. We haven't had his IQ tested but he is clearly smart. Every report card has been great. We call eighth grade his rock star year. He put himself in for the running of class president and won. He grew his hair out, again, careful what you wish for. We wanted him to express his own identity and here it was. He became more social. He started having movie nights at the house with his friends. I thought one day, here all I wanted was for life to be tolerable and here it was, insanely good.

In his speech at the end of eighth grade he said he was very prepared for high school. I sat there and thought, yes you are. In every way and ways I never thought you would be.

High school?

Going into high school was another juncture. We decided to let him decide where he wanted to go. We talked about it being his thing. He had the option of public high school, a coeducational private school or two military schools. He went to see the schools. He thought the coed private school was just an extension of junior high and he wanted something different. He went to the public school and realized he wanted prayer involved. When that came into play I thought if that had become a tool for him, he needs that. The religious school had given him a framework that worked for him. Then he picked a Christian military school and it just worked for him. It was clear at this school how you wore your uniform, how you walk down the hall, how you address teachers, and all the kids have to do it that way so he no longer stood out. In fact, he's applauded for doing it right.

He decided freshman year that he wanted to play football. Never played football a day in his life. Off he went. He is in all these high level courses and he has quite a load. I thought

I had better really watch his stress this year. Then we got his report card and he was doing great and he seems great.

When he was invited to a prom I thought I needed to tell him this is what you do, this is what you say. Then he came home and told me it wasn't that much fun. The girl had come and was very nervous acting and I watched him try to calm her. He told me that he started talking to another girl who was very chatty. That was who he took to his prom. I never would have thought he would be drawn to that sort of girl. Once again, he surprised me.

Crystal ball from now?

Now I ask myself, what is he going to cure! He's got a mind that whatever he decides to do he will be so successful at it I can't even imagine. I am no longer surprised with anything my son comes home to tell me he's done or offered to do. Do I have any concerns? I'll probably never stop. I'm his mother. I still am concerned about stress and how he handles it. He's still quiet but affectionate in his own ways.

He has no limits.

Final comments?

We used to comment on the top ten things people say when you tell them your child has autism. (1) Be thankful it's not cancer. Which I was. I get what people were saying but I wouldn't say that to someone now. (2) God doesn't give you what you can't handle. Which I wanted to respond to with God doesn't see me curled up in the corner then because I'm not handling it. I'm screaming at a small child with autism because I can't handle him. I would say to people, find the people who will help you.

We had some tough years but I am so grateful for where Bobby is now, where we all are now. I have a different appreciation for some very basic things. You have a kid out there running a race. Do you care if they win? No. They're in life.

Excerpts from an eighth grade graduation speech, by Bobby

We have learned so much over our years in this school. Tonight I am going to talk about the three things that I think are the most important to this school: faith, academics, and friendship.

Faith is defined in the Bible as "the assurance of things hoped for and the conviction of things not seen." The dictionary simply says faith is "belief in and loyalty to God." Anyone at this school knows that faith means so much more than that. Bobby goes on to describe faith displayed through daily prayer, food donations, a giving tree, cards to nursing home residents, wall hanging biblical quotes, and ultimately, faith is the conviction of the things not seen, but we do see faith first hand.

Academics are obviously important. We have been blessed with teachers. Bobby goes on to cite teachers' individual gifts with humor. He comments that his library teacher, *learned us real good at grammar and now we is really smart.* And to his math teacher, *What would we do without knowing the Dewey Decimal system?* After listing his current teachers he reflects: *But there is one more teacher that I want to mention. I've heard the saying that everything you need to know in life you learn in kindergarten. I'm pretty lucky because I couldn't have had a better kindergarten teacher. Thank you Mrs H. You always understood why I wanted everything organized and why I wanted my crayons in alphabetical order. Probably that's because yours were too.*

The last thing I want to talk about is friendship. Nine years ago many of us walked into this building for the first time. There was a lot of apprehension, a lot of crying, and a lot of not letting go of the car door handles. But when our parents finally stopped all their nonsense, we were able to get to know each other and start forming friendships.

Bobby concluded with:

I just want to say how lucky I am to have spent these years of my life with such an incredible group of people. As you go on to high school, remember to always have fun, be yourself, and don't stop believing.

Amy

Amy pulled her chair up to the table. Her eyes met mine for a brief moment and she smiled. This may not seem like a big deal to many, but my heart warmed at the friendly expression from my loved friend. I have known Amy over many years and have watched her grow with the challenges of autistic spectrum disorder. She is now 13 years old.

I first met Amy when I was asked to consult to a classroom for a child who was "wreaking havoc" by refusing to enter the classroom, hiding under her desk, and huddling with her knees wrapped in her arms for much of the school day. This child had some good language skill in very low stimulating environments, but had poor social connection. Her expression was flat; she had little interest in the other children, and appeared distraught to be in this regular education setting. This child, however, was quite bright and was managing to do grade level academically. The challenge to this consultant was to help get her behaviors under control and help support better social understanding so that she would be more available to learn in the social setting of the regular classroom. No one wanted to see her fail there as she appeared to have so much potential.

This child was Amy and she has had a profound impact on my understanding of autism. Her perseverance and spirit have greatly impacted my view of human development. I am grateful for my time with her over the years, and for this amazing interview.

Tell me about yourself Amy.

"I like many kinds of TV shows and sometimes I like acting them out. I like pretending that I am actually in shows. That's really fun for me."

How old are you now?

"I'm 13 and I've had my autism ever since I was born. I didn't even know it when I was like five. I found out when I was nine or ten years old. My mom told me, and get this; no one in my family was autistic before me. It was really weird."

What do you think about autism?

"I think it is kind of a gift and a curse. I don't understand things as plainly as other kids do. Like, if they say something complicated I sometimes can't understand it."

I asked for an example. Like tough math equations for high schoolers or something. I tried to clarify the thoughts. "Tough math equations are complicated, but give me an example of something other kids might say that is hard to understand. I wouldn't understand the type of autism, I'm not sure." Amy seemed confused by her own initial comment. The concept was restated. "It's hard to understand, let me think," pause, "when things truly are my autism it's hard for me to blend in. I stick out too much."

What sticks out? "Well, not all the plugs in my brain are plugged in correctly. And, I see things others don't clearly see. I'm really sensitive to some things." Amy starts to fidget and pull out strands of her hair, a habit that has come to indicate that she is getting stressed or bored. She is reassured that she is doing a good job and she is focused again.

You mentioned that you see things differently.

"Sometimes I see images in my head like my favorite cartoon characters. They make me feel stronger and help me get through my day."

How do they help you?

"They make me think that I'll be going to see them when I get home." She points to two beat-up old dolls of animation characters on the chair behind her. This interviewer remembers the many plans and strategies that had been put in place over the years to decrease her perseverations on them and her repeated attempt to bring them to school despite the social inappropriateness as she got older. "They calm me. If anything ever happened to them I don't know what I'd do."

How is it different from when you get home you know that your mom is there?

"Mom has always been there for me since the day of my birth. She been supporting me all these years and I am very grateful to her, very grateful."

Has your mom had to do anything different for you because you're autistic?

"She has to help me organize. I can't do that well. I have a hard time concentrating and I can go off into my own world and my mom pulls me back. I've realized she has been doing this since I was seven or eight years old. A lot of people have helped pull me back."

How is your world different than the world your mom and I are in?

"My world is kind of a place that I dream would really happen. No violence, no swear words no anything is there, nothing bad is there."

Who is in that world?

"I don't know about people being there. I want my cartoon characters. I do know that wouldn't be real if people weren't there. I want to become a scientist when I get older and I hope to build a portal that would bridge the two worlds. I could hook it up to a computer and hold up a cartoon I want to see and I could step through. My dream would be to have the portal that would go between my autistic world and the real world. My creatures and people could be together, even though my Mom says these things aren't real, there's this feeling I get when I see the characters that I know and love. I could take other people there so that they would know what I mean and understand autism a little."

What else about being autistic do you think makes you stick out, as you said before?

"I pull at my hair a lot."

Does it bother you when people stop you?

"No, it helps me get rid of damaged hair and dandruff." The question is clarified. "No it doesn't bother me; people just don't want me to go bald. I also often gaze out into space just dreaming the day away. I do have to say I am a great artist."

"Sometimes I stick out with girls too. In my girls group sometimes I get a little out of control. I can get hyper and have trouble listening to anyone."

What makes that happen?

"If someone is threatening me, being mean, or just being annoying. Yelling is threatening, fighting is threatening. I don't like when people don't get along. It's like I feel their pain, I can see their pain. It's like I'm having the fight myself and I get scared and angry all together. I don't like when people use swear words."

What do you think is annoying?

"My brother. My sister when she's being mean. But she's actually really nice. My mom is annoying when she gets up in everyone's business. The world can annoy me. It's kind of ruining my dream, the portal that I mentioned a few minutes ago. And, well, I don't like the swear words. Hate really bothers me. If people stopped hating we would live in a better world."

Does anything bother you that you don't think bothers other people?

"If I sit too long, my butt hurts. I don't like when people say random things. I don't like when girls I know get really upset about assignments. A boy I know, he's shirking in his work a bit. I am bothered by that. I have very sensitive ears. Sometimes the volume of the room can bother me. Loud noise can bother me."

Give me an example of loud noise.

She screams, literally. Accurate answer to a stupid question.

"My skin is very sensitive. It can burn a little bit. I am very sensitive about shots. Do shots hurt you?" She asks me.

"They said it was going to hurt like a bee sting but it was really not like that."

"Sometimes I'm alone by myself and I talk to myself a lot. I'll do episodes of total drama action. When I'm alone I can be a little sad. I want my cartoon characters. Sometimes I want my mom or my friend, she has autism too. Whenever I'm lonely I go to the computer or to the piano."

Tell me about friends.

"There was a boy that used to call me a freak. He even made fun of my family. He said mean things. I used to not know how to act. I wanted to just clobber him. Now I can just ignore him. I really love my family."

"My friends are my cartoon characters but I know they are not real. Sally is my real friend. She likes things that I like but she is a little different to me. She likes anime and other stuff, like naruto. She likes Japanese stuff. She shops at Hot Topics. I started to shop there after I met her and I got a T-shirt there."

"I have another friend. How about we have a sleep over?" She asks her mother. "My brother and sister always have friends over and I never do. Why? Because it's hard to get in contact with people who like me. People who like me for who I am?"

What do you think about your autism?

"I like my autism. It helps me create and do things no one else can do. Just this morning, when the door was locked. I inspected it and took a paper clip to unlock it. I came up with a different idea than the key the teacher was using. I know the lock was stuck inside."

How do you want high school to be?

"I want to join a swimming club that would let me swim for fun. And, when I turn 16 I think I want to get my drivers permit and audition for American Idol. Maybe I'll become an artist."

Is that something you think you'd like to do when you're grown up?

"Yes, be an artist. Maybe draw cartoons. But I also think I'd like to work with kids like me. The parents could tell me what they need and I could help them. My autism isn't going to hurt me. But some people today don't accept autistic kids. One time, this kid couldn't go bowling because this other kid said I don't want to be with that autistic kid. I don't want to see things like that."

"Of course my autism won't stop me from doing anything. Autism is not just a condition. It's a part of who you are and what you want to do with yourself."

"I'm pretty much done now."

And, she was.

The mother's response

The mother comments.

I am amazed at how she is able to see herself. I think she sees herself more clearly than we do. We still want to protect her. She really is so much more capable than we ever thought.

Did her answers surprise you?

I thought she was more lonely. I didn't realize how much conflict affects her, but she misperceives disagreements and gets very upset be little arguments. She thinks anything is yelling. Sometimes even when someone is excited she is disarmed. That's a weakness, gauging emotional responses is hard for her. The non-verbal part of interacting confuses her.

Tell me about Amy as a baby and young child. When did you recognize something was different about her?

Immediately. Within the first month or two. She didn't look at me when I nursed. Then she never looked for me in a room. I could leave her anywhere and I'd find her in the same place. I could leave her with anyone and she wouldn't even look back for me.

When did you start to really be concerned?

Originally I thought she was deaf. Her affect was so flat and she didn't respond to her name. We went for a hearing test and then at about one-year-old we saw a pediatrician who said children develop at different rates. Two months later we saw a developmental pediatrician who said she was autistic. We still were convinced she was deaf. Before the visit I went on the internet and saw things about autism but she didn't rock or bang her head so I eliminated that. I thought the internet was really frightening.

What was your response to the diagnosis?

You're shattered. I felt I couldn't fix it. I felt hopeless. I had a two-year-old and I worried about what kind of life she was going to have. I had just had a new baby boy and I thought how will I handle this? And they said this was genetic and it was far more likely in boys. I thought, this is just the beginning. My husband handled it much better than I did. He felt things were going to be okay while I was up with anxiety at night.

Then I mobilized. I called everyone I knew who knew anyone who knew anyone who knew anything about autism. I spent the first few months calling every single person I knew. I met some really amazing mothers. I'll never forget one mother who at the height of my apprehension I met, who had a child with autism. She said to me, "Are you okay?" I said, "No." She said, "But you will be." She was the only person up until that point who asked me that. Many people didn't know what to say to me. Part of that is the anguish other people are feeling. They don't know how to support you.

That is the most horrible time. When you walk out of that office with the diagnosis. If they had told me she had some kind of cancer I would have been able to call the medical establishment and asked who's the best doctor. Where do I go? What do I do? As a parent at that point, you are not steered in any direction. No one could tell me what the best options were. It wasn't guided. I was terrified.

So, we started by enrolling her in an intense program. My heart is still with that preschool. When you get them into a program like that, it changes your whole life. People came into our house everyday. Those people are still like family to us. After a little while she started to vocalize. They taught us not to make excuses for her behaviors. "Oh, she's autistic let her be." She would make a peep and we would run to her. We learned that we had to ignore tantrums instead of attend to them. We learned what to ignore and how to address behaviors. We learned how to extinguish behaviors. Amy would rip paper all the time so one day they spent the whole day ripping paper and it extinguished.

Slowly, you start to live a life. One day you're eating at a restaurant and you recognize, here we are. She can sit at a table and she can make it through a whole dinner. The moments come slowly, but they come.

Do you find those moments now when you find yourself doing something you didn't think you'd be able to do?

I do. I think it's hard as a parent to look at the positive things that have occurred and not always look at what you have to work on. I have a difficult time with that. I'm always driven to fix things. I'm always watching her and problem solving instead of saying, look at her take part of an activity I never thought I'd be seeing her do. I don't know if it's just a mother thing. I think it's heightened for her though.

Did you try any treatment courses early on?

Chiropractics. My husband felt strongly that it helped. I didn't see any harm in it. I called a holistic person and was going to start various vitamins and then didn't. We tried the diet without any response really. She is not a kid who had any signs of gut or digestive problems and I think maybe those children benefit from the diet path.

How did you feel when she entered the school age years?

I cried my eyes out. I hated to see her leave her preschool. I didn't think anything would be the same. She wouldn't be safe or protected. We took her to the kindergarten program to see it and I just cried. I thought this is where it falls apart.

I saw other children standing in line, listening to the teachers, watching each other. I thought she'd never fit in there. The teacher reminded me that I was looking at children who had been in kindergarten for a year. It was May and she said these children had come a long way.

So, Amy went into kindergarten and she actually did okay. She had aide support and did all right.

First grade was tough because they were expected to sit in their seats and they couldn't move around. She didn't have enough freedom to move around. I'll say this forever, the teacher you have is the most important piece to success each year. The core teacher is the core of the program. Unless you have a teacher who is willing to be flexible and to bend a little, you're done. They need to be able to not take the behaviors personally. If a power struggle ensues it never works out.

She started to run out of the room and out of the school. She had real escape behaviors. She was very active and just couldn't attend to the lessons or the behavior plans. I remember the day I spoke to the doctor about it. I described her running to the windows. The teachers thought she was trying to escape. The doctor sat and talked to her and to us about it and it was revealed that she was anxious about getting home again. She had a lot of anxiety symptoms. She had a lot of irrational fears and then we started to see that anxiety was really blocking her. We talked and talked to her doctors about it and made the decision to try a medication. Just to focus on the anxiety piece. Here we were, dead set against medications thinking that was a cop out. When she was younger we said to each other that if we had to consider medication then the programs had failed. And, worse, we had failed her. Now I realize how foolish that was.

What did the doctor say to convince you to try a medication trial?

He asked, "If she were a diabetic would you give her insulin?" "Would you like to be inside her and feel what she seems to be feeling?" "Would you want to live with the intensity of those feelings?" So we tried it and she responded really nicely to the medication. Within a month we saw a marked improvement in her anxiety levels. She was much better able to manage herself in school. But then her inattention was revealed and an attention medication was tried. That change was like night and day. I am convinced that is the reason she was able to stay in the school system. It really allowed her to be able to function in a regular classroom. Medications are such a scary issue and I don't want to make light of it to other parents. The people you talk to forget that this is not anything you as a parent are familiar with or comfortable discussing. You don't know the lingo and you are scared to death that you are going to make the wrong decision for your child. That was the hardest part for me I think. The fear of the wrong decision was huge, we were afraid of choosing the wrong program or trying the wrong meds. Every decision felt so life or death in the early years.

Did you ever feel like things weren't moving forward?

When she was in third or fourth grade we went to the Mall one night. Her older sister wanted to get her ears pierced for her birthday. The whole family went to the Mall and something set Amy off. She lay down on the floor and tried to kick the glass out of the front of a store. I looked at my husband and thought, "What is this about? We're just at the Mall?" And then I looked over at my pre-adolescent older daughter and she looked completely humiliated. She looked like she wanted to disappear and it just broke my heart. My husband picked her up and took her to the car. That day the fear came back.

But we are fortunate because Amy likes to join in with family activities and we just told her that if she acted like that she would not be able to come. The fact that she's motivated to be with us is a very positive thing. We are able to say, "You will act like this or you will not come," and it usually works.

Any moments of real joy?

Many. Amy played the piano in a recital. She walked right up to the stage and did great. When she walked up to a child who was playing a sport and fell and she told him it would be okay. She's very kind. She amazed us everyday. There are so many times I am just amazed at her. It's so hard to be alone, to see her so alone. It hurts me that I can't fix that. I can't make friends for her. But she gets up and goes on everyday with a great attitude. She's very positive. She'll come home and tell a positive story everyday. Even if it's just about something she ate.

How are you different as a mother today?

Wow. [Pause, and then in jest]: I think every child should go through ABA. She's my only child who actually listens to anything I say. Seriously, when I'm with my other two children at an event, like a game or something, and I see parents who are so, "My kid is No.1" and all that. And I think to myself, you should be considering yourself lucky that the kid is healthy and able to be a part of all this. We all fall into that parent thing where you meet someone and you start reading your child's resumé. "My child is a straight A student, my child is captain of the football team, my child is going to a prestigious college." I really think the competition these children face is so difficult today. With my other two kids, that's the only conversation I have with other parents. When you attend something with parents of kids with disabilities you realize how much of the other stuff is ridiculous nonsense. To have a happy healthy child who is able to relate to the world, just be thrilled with that! But again, you can't expect people to understand what they haven't had to understand. I don't judge them. I may have been just like those other parents if I hadn't had Amy.

Does it change how you parent your other kids?

Absolutely. I'm very proud of the kids. They are very sensitive to any child with a disability or any need. They really stand up for their sister. I also value my other kids' experiences in the world. And, when they bring it back and share it with you. I don't get those from her. I know there are times when my other two children just want it to be about them. They'll say why is it always about autism. Our family feels fractured at these times. Then there are times when we are the strongest unit in the world around her. I think it fluctuates for the other kids.

When you think back to when she was two, what did you see ahead?

I thought she would be in a school only for autistic children. I didn't see her going out of the house with the other two kids. I thought we would need heavy duty supports. I didn't think she would have any language. At that point she was so disconnected. She didn't even seem to see me as her mother. When she was five I thought we were dead in the water. I thought to myself, "How am I going to conform this child to fit this system?" My worst fear was how to find a place for her in this world. There are only so many days when you can go to the door to pick up your child and you hear your child did this and this. You just get so worn down.

At eight to ten years old we were in the height of behaviors. I was putting out fires everyday. That was the toughest physical piece of raising her those years. But, the academic piece became strong so I had more hope. I had something to latch on to. Then at 12 to 15, it was much better than I ever expected. Never thought we would settle into the rhythm that we're in. I never would have pictured her getting on the bus by herself, or waiting for the late bus after school if she stayed for an activity. I didn't think she would be calmly able to express to us what she needed or wanted.

Where do you see the future now?

I think she'll do fine in high school. She may even do better because she'll find her niche. I see that coming. I think I would like to see her try college. I would like to see her use that creativity piece she's so proud of. I still have to give her a lot of cues about basic things. Sometimes on the weekend I am aware of how much I have to do to help her get into the day, prodding for her to get showered, dressed etc. I guess I am optimistic that she'll live on her own one day. But I'm also realistic enough to have plan B. Maybe she will need supports.

I am amazed that she has come this far. I think we're always afraid that the progress will stop. We ask ourselves, "Is this as good as it's going to get?" But then she keeps growing. She just keeps surprising us.

Final comments?

I have to say that the diagnosis is not half as bad as you think it's going to be when they hand it to you. It's really important for parents to not be ashamed. I see parents who hide it, or can't face it and deal with it. I am really thankful to whatever force in the universe that I didn't go that way. We were lucky, my husband and I functioned as a team from day one. He has been an immense support and I am so thankful that he is the person standing with me on this unexpected journey. I am so blessed we are able to say this is who she is and you know what, this is okay. This is more than okay. She is a gift.

Bill

You will see as you read this text that Bill is a very articulate young man who is able to share ideas openly. He also happens to have Asperger's syndrome. Bill was quite interested in sharing his story, as he wants people to appreciate children with Asperger's for who they are rather than the label assigned to them. This teenager is defining his identity, as they all do, but with great introspection and extro-spect, a term he coined himself. He commented that there should be an opposite of introspection and he defines it as being sensitive to others from the outside. He'll explain his perspectives better than I. Meet Bill.

"I'm just me"

I am 15 years old and I have Asperger's syndrome. I didn't know about it until later in life when I was 12. My mother knew when I was ten and I wish she told me earlier. Nothing against her, just I would have liked to know. We were standing in the kitchen and she just told me straight out. It was actually really good to know. I needed to tell people that something was different. I read about it and conformed myself into it a little. If I read about something someone with Asperger's did, I did it. I started waving it in faces. I thought, "you can't blame me for something, I have Asperger". He goes on to describe that he might have said statement perceived as rude and people would get mad at him. He liked the "scapegoat" of the label he later shared. I think maybe I wanted sympathy after the diagnosis too. This is a phase that went away over time. But I think when some people hear they have Asperger's they get better because they have been ridiculed so much they try not to ridicule others; unless they never learned because they were ridiculed too much and they became bitter. When I heard I had the diagnosis, at that time I didn't know I was arrogant. I just thought I was smart and better than everybody else. It, the diagnosis, took me down a notch. After a while I thought, I'm just me. Getting diagnosed gave me a solid place to start self-awareness. It gave me a foundation.

"I get on a roll"

A lot of time, I'm joking and everybody is laughing. Then I run out of funny things, then I put out okay jokes and then I start putting out ridiculous jokes. I get going and I can't stop. I get really confident. What I wanted to say to everybody is, "Hey, if I say anything weird or out there it's not me, it's Asperger's." Asked if he felt criticized or put down: People weren't mean to me. In sixth grade, as the grades got higher, people actually got nicer. It was hard thought. I liked this girl in fifth grade. I was affectionate. Bill is asked to clarify what affectionate meant. I talked about how much I liked her all the time, and to her. I was harassing her. She didn't like it and she ran away. I was on a roll and couldn't stop myself. Then when I cooled down and it was pointed out to me, I knew I did this or that wrong. I tried subtle attention next. Asked to clarify subtle attention but he couldn't remember.

Bill starts telling me about his current girlfriend. I met my new girlfriend at a camp. We became best friends. I hadn't paid that much attention to my social life. But we started talking and became good friends. She is very sensitive. We see each other on weekends and we write on the computer. We talk on the phone every night. My mom doesn't let me text.

What is Asperger syndrome to you?

I view Asperger's not as something that you have, it is what you are. What does someone without Asperger's have? If they came up with a medicine they would be enhanced rather than conform to normalcy? What is a "typical" person? If someone had more social ability they wouldn't get a label. Everybody has differences. Everybody literally has some genetic mutation. But then culture splits them into groups. People can get stereotyped. "Normal" means there is a scale of what is and is not "normal." "Typical" becomes based on the population. The idea here is that those with Asperger's are humans, only a different type of human.

Share what you think is different in your perspective

I've noticed that I am on the cusp of Asperger's. I was so misled on the social scene but it has developed in a way that I am not exactly Asperger's but I'm not exactly not Asperger's. I think when anyone on the autistic spectrum is stressed they go further into their own world. When I get really embarrassed or something I make a sound and do this thing with my hand. It's a compulsive feeling and I shut off. It's a far-fetched idea, but maybe that's the reason that people further down the spectrum are more shut out. I see that with other kids I know. But they can look back on it. I think most people with Asperger's can look back at what they do. Whatever AS did to me it caused me to be who I am today. Even the bad parts form my character. It has molded me to who I am and I wouldn't take away, because it would change whom I am. Now, some with more severe AS get broken instead of molded I think.

"I like myself"

I do like the person I am today. I always sort of liked who I am. I never stopped liking myself but I sometimes disliked what I did. I never really knew Asperger's and I had nothing to blame, so I blamed the universe. Back to when I first was told that I had Asperger's, I tried to be Asperger's. I guess that was just a phase. I think a lot of people with AS would conform to the label. Now I think the best thing is to act naturally. If you don't feel like laughing, don't laugh. If every time someone wrote LOL (laughing out loud) on the computer they actually laughed, that would be ridiculous.

A friend

I think you need to let things happen to you until you know more about yourself. Then you have enough skills to get out there more. You really can't have friends at school unless you trust yourself. Unless you find someone who is your level (socially). I can't break out in school. I am pretty much to myself there. I have acquaintances. How do you differentiate a friend from an acquaintance? A friend is someone I would like to get up to do something for. I have a friend I would give a video game because I would like to see how he thinks about it later. It is that interest in the other person and that you want to share something. You need to find people outside of school that are more like yourself. You need to get out and do things. I met my friends at a camp, and I go to a social group on Friday nights.

Tell me more about AS

Asperger's is basically a social-developmental problem and the rest, the emotional problems; the awkwardness etc. comes from living in life as Asperger's. You're basically like play dough that comes out that tube and molds you. At first as a little kid, it's tough. When you're a little kid and everybody is not so socially developed and other kids don't understand that you have feelings too. And, you don't understand that other people have feelings. It will take a little longer for someone with AS to understand that. At around eight years old I actually got feelings for other people. I recognized that I felt bad for doing something to someone.

Another part of this topic is the fact that you have to think about everything you say, it really helps in mental development; just thinking hard helps intellectual development. Another positive thing is that people with AS are often very sensitive, though you wouldn't necessarily see that. If there were a big crowd rushing in to something, you would see someone with AS standing outside. And, what you get from being put down goes into EXTRO-SPECT. [Asked to clarify]. It's the opposite of introspection. Instead of self-analyzing you other analyze. It just makes sense. I don't really understand personalities, I understand behaviors.

Hyper-focus

One positive thing is the focusing thing. It opens up a lot of stress relieving activities. Sometimes when you hyper-focus simple things make you happy. I can better explain the happiness caused by simple things by explaining the unhappiness caused by complex things. Complex things are awkward situations and unknown situations. Some hard things can be simple, like if someone likes to do math they can hyper-focus on math and it makes the world simpler.

Interests

I like mental concepts, the twilight zone sort of thing. Thinking about things in different ways. I like psychology. Talking to other people helps me organize my thoughts. Even right now I am learning more about myself. I used to be interested in video games. I don't like physical things, that I know of.

Challenges

If I get sick I can really get thrown off. I get all unmotivated. Change from holidays can get to me. If plans are changed I'm okay now. When I was little it really bothered me. I like physical change, like when we change my room around. It takes me a little bit to get used to it but then I like it. I also used to obsess about what was going to happen next but I'm better now. If I want something done though, I want to do it right then and there.

I've noticed...

I've noticed that typical people don't notice details as well as I do. And, they talk a lot less.

The future

I have goals. They are very assuming. As in "I assume this will happen and then..." Mostly I want to be some sort of counselor. I want to learn about psychology.

I think it's really important that you have someone to say everything to. You need someone you can tell anything to. You need to work on empathy and sensitivity to others. Empathy is that you can understand others. Sensitivity is that you don't want to hurt them. You need to practice too. Once I said someone was fat, just as an observation. They were large. I didn't mean anything by it. Mom said, "That's rude." I stopped because I realized people don't like that.

Final comment

I really recommend that children with AS get into social groups and build a network. I am doing a leadership program and I go to a program on Friday nights. Most of us are socially successful. But to be in social situations can be exhausting.

"Stimming" is good stuff. Just flicking a string calms me. Exercise can really help too. It helps with sorting out irrational from rational thoughts. Irrational thoughts are often worries.

People with Asperger's need to know that most people who ridicule them have worse problems than they do. Ninety-nine percent of the time, their issues are bigger than your own. Just ignore them. Be happy with who you are.

It is delightful to see Bill so happy with who he is!

Danny

Danny's mother enthusiastically agreed to share their story for this edition. Parenting Danny took a twist as he was diagnosed with a pervasive developmental disorder. Not what these parent expected to be challenged by, but they took the challenge on just the same with compassion, love and commitment. Danny is making terrific strides and his mother delights as she shares their story.

What were you anticipating when you were first expecting?

I had a wonderful pregnancy. I felt so healthy and I loved the way my body looked. I knew just what I was supposed to do and I did everything. I exercised almost every day of the pregnancy. I didn't eat fish. I loved being pregnant and felt such a connection to Danny. I think I felt myself becoming a mom when I was pregnant. I felt myself changing. I was just in love with him. It was one of the happiest times in my life.

The delivery was wonderful. I had an epidural. My uncle was the doctor that delivered Danny. We had lots of family in the delivery room. It was like he came out into a Sunday dinner. It was wonderful. I couldn't wait to get pregnant again right after that.

It was hard the first couple months. One reason was I only breast fed and never pumped. I nursed him for 18 months. I was tired but I felt natural being a mom. It was like I forgot the life I had before. I felt like he gave me a purpose and I had such a rich life. I loved it.

His first year was good. We had some personal issues in our marriage that first year and I recognize now that stress made me less aware of some of the things Danny did or didn't do. I feel that having a baby can magnify any stresses a marriage may have. It's easy to be a couple and live somewhat independent lives. Then all of a sudden I became a mom. I had higher expectations for myself, my marriage, my new family. Tensions rose and it was a difficult time. We've worked things out and we have a much stronger relationship.

Aside from the stress in the marriage I felt that Danny was doing fine. Looking back now I see some things. After the initial diagnosis I started to think of things in that first year. Now I have a five-month-old and it is so different with her. I see things now that I know Danny didn't do in the first year. When I would change his diaper he didn't really engage in your face but he would respond to words. He seemed really into words. He wouldn't laugh and giggle at social games, like peek a boo. But he would giggle at certain words, particularly long words or Italian words that sounded different. I knew from when he was four to five months that he loved words. At the time we thought it was cute. I thought we were having a connection but for him it was about the words.

As we progressed through the first year I did all the nursery rhymes and he seemed to like it. After the diagnosis I tried just humming some of the games and he didn't seem to know what I was doing, even with the hand motions. As soon as I put the words to it he would respond. He didn't realize that the main purpose of the game was the social connection, he was into the words. When he was six months old he would look at the words in books. He would smile at you but he just wasn't very animated. His range of expression is not close to what my five-month-old can do.

When were you first concerned?

He did everything he was supposed to developmentally just not as much as we thought he should. There was not something that I thought he couldn't do at all. The summer before his second birthday we were driving down the road and he started picking out letters on signs. He was pointing from his car seat to letters. It became more and more obvious that that was what stood out to him in the world. It was as if the rest of the world was black and white and letters were neon. Also, he wasn't talking to me. He could say lots of things but he talked at you. He would use you to meet his needs, but there wasn't really any conversation. Around two we were more concerned. We knew he was very bright. He seemed to be grasping things other toddlers wouldn't come up with like "The possum is upside down." When he woke up at night it was as if he couldn't turn his mind off. He started to obsess over movies. Every time we watched movies it had to be Peter Pan. He was very self-directed. He would rather play with the remote control than most other things. He would watch with us or his grandfather and he would hold his hand or lay across us. But, he didn't seem to really be sharing the experience. He was taken with the images on the screen, not so much the story. As soon as we got the diagnosis we stopped watching television. We use it very rarely and now he will say to me, "Is that shark bad? This is scary." He is more interactive and will share.

His first experience with preschool

I took him to Montessori because that was what I had wanted for my kids. I was behind a two-way mirror and I watched as a teacher was trying to give him a little assessment. It was right in front of my face that he was entirely self-directed. He didn't have bad behavior, he just wasn't following along with her at all. He completely ignored her and once he found the letter and number puzzle the teacher basically didn't exist to him. I hadn't noticed how bad the eye contact was at that point. The teacher came in to tell me that she couldn't assess him, which had been obvious to me. So I went home and called a relative who was a speech therapist and I told her what had happened. She shared that she didn't think that his eye contact was very good. She had seen him engaged with people but she felt that unless you were doing something right in his face he didn't really respond. She suggested that I have him evaluated. She put out a bunch of things one of which was high functioning autism. Then I talked to someone at a developmental office and I told her about how Danny had lined up all these miniature animals in a line through the house. It was disturbing and I wanted to throw them across the room. That nurse told me that there were red flags and we set up an appointment.

Before the appointment I went to the book store and got 11 books and had read them before I saw the developmental pediatrician. I stopped working so he wouldn't have to be with the nanny. The nanny we had pretty much just followed him around and let him do whatever he wanted. He had someone there to just meet his every need. I decided to be there to make sure he got out. I took him out to socialize more to see how he would be. I saw that he just wasn't connecting to the world. Something was in his way.

The doctor's visit

By the time I got there I figured that doctor would say it was autistic spectrum disorder. I thought I would get a diagnosis that day but I was hoping he wouldn't, that maybe he was so high functioning he wouldn't be able to call it. I was so afraid of a label, and I felt shame. I didn't want anything to be wrong with my child. I wanted to be in denial but you just can't be. You just wanted the nightmare to not be happening. I had started to see all his idiosyncrasies so much more clearly. I became resentful of things he did because it was autism glaring me in the face. I couldn't even blow dry my hair because I felt I had to spend my waking hours keeping him from doing behaviors that looked autistic. If I was drying my hair he would line up toys so I just tried to keep him occupied all the time.

The doctor did diagnose him with mild autism. He drew a chart and said everybody responds differently to treatment. He said we needed to follow how he develops and we would see more over time. It was a sad time. You have to grieve the normal process. You have to acknowledge that you're not going to go on play dates and have wine in the corner with the other mothers as you may have imagined. You get the grief and you move past it.

Starting therapy

By the time I had gone to see the doctor I had already read about different therapies. I was drawn to one that talked about emotional connection. I wanted desperately for him to really experience life and have a full life. I felt so helpless as a parent. I had tried to play blocks with him as he just kept throwing the blocks and I just sat there and cried. I didn't know why he was doing it or how to make him stop. It killed me that I didn't understand what made my son tick. I went to see different programs. The thought of dropping him off at a program was very overwhelming to me so I wanted some place that he would be nurtured. One program seemed to really get him and he was placed in an integrated classroom that offered some peers to model after even though he wasn't really responding to any other kids at that point. I liked that he would have a chance to connect to other kids.

After he got into the early intervention programming my husband and I went to a training on relationship development intervention (RDI). We had to really look at our schedules and how we would share the responsibilities. This was defining for us as a family. We had to deal with it head on together. We were both open to the strategies. From the conference we were connected with a therapist who would help us more directly. We started a lengthy assessment process and then made a plan. We kept him in programming because we liked the social models. I would work with him throughout the week constantly and started keeping him home one day. We were mindful of what was going on and we wanted him to keep the speech therapy as well. But at home we started the RDI. We took out talking to him so much. For two weeks we were quiet and we would only talk when he would look at us and then we would reinforce it with hugging or tickling. We made it obvious to Danny what we wanted from him. It was as if he didn't know what we wanted. We created gaps so that he had to look for us and then gave an exaggerated response. In the beginning you feel like a loon. But he needed that because he just didn't get things naturally. After a few weeks we saw improved eye contact. He slowly wanted to do things with me. In everything we did I gave him a specific role and made it clear to him what he was to do; such as giver, taker, sprayer, washer. Once you start thinking like that you can break the whole world down into units. We would do windows and I would wipe and then Danny would spray cleaner. I would take the laundry out and he would put it in. We had to bring the world down to the beginning stages and make that invisible string to us. We knew within a couple of weeks that we were doing the right thing.

He is now in an integrated classroom. He was in the specialized program for about six months, but we eventually moved him out because we felt that in the program he was prompted too much and we wanted him to think more for himself.

The doctor sees tremendous gains

The diagnosis of autism was removed when we returned to the doctor several months later. Danny no longer fit the diagnostic criteria for an autistic spectrum disorder. The core deficit of social impairment had improved significantly. The mother is asked to comment on this. I do think there are still abnormalities. When there are a lot of people around or we're in a new environment he is off the wall. Now would you look at him and say he's autistic, no. You might think he was over excited. His teachers have told me that you have to be a teacher and really watch him to see his challenges. He is not fully into social play to the extent that other children his age are. He still would rather talk to adults than children. We focus on keeping him interested and engaged in life. We try to find the areas of life that he feels passionate about and when that happens I think that friends will come. Our focus this year is to keep him engaged socially even when the teachers aren't around. I feel that the diagnosis, or maybe just tendencies, may become more relevant again. It is part of who Danny is and we have to accept him for who he is. I feel that his brain is such a gift but it is imbalanced. It needs to be guided. We have a big job as parents. The world is his oyster but we better be on top of our game raising him. He's been given wonderful gifts but with those gifts is responsibility for us. I might not have to work on letters and numbers with him but I know his areas of need and I'll work on them.

What do you think is ahead now?

I try really hard to not have a crystal ball. I try to appreciate him for who he is. When it becomes too hard for him to be at a family party we go for ice cream. I try not to judge what other people have against what I have. I am thankful that I have kids that are healthy and can talk to me. Danny is such a special human being and I have faith that his life will be wonderful. I don't want to put my concept of what wonderful is for us on him. I want to focus on being the best parent I can be for him.

Christopher

Christopher is an older child with Asperger syndrome. Like so many children with Asperger's, the collection of his developmental differences didn't spell out any particular disorder until later in his life. Certainly, Jan, his mother, recognized Chris' struggles early on, and she has worked instinctively to help him along his path of growing up. She has sought the support of many professionals throughout his life, yet only recently had him diagnosed with Asperger syndrome. This is their story told by Jan.

Chris was born outside of this United States and was nine weeks premature. He had a life-threatening heart condition and our total focus for his first few years of life was around that. When he was two weeks old he had apneic episodes (periods of not breathing) and he had an echo (a diagnostic test of heart function). It was amazing there because they didn't have a lot of medical equipment so they had to be really good diagnosticians. Chris was treated and had surgery by the age of two. When he was in the hospital following his surgery I asked for an orthopedic consult because he wasn't hitting his motor milestones. He didn't roll over, sit up, or start to walk as expected. And, he didn't pursue toys out of reach. My strong intuition told me that there was more to this than just the cardiac stuff. The ortho doctor told me essentially to relax. I was an older mother and he thought that I was over-reacting. My husband had to just about restrain me. I knew something wasn't right. I said, "Well, I'm going to keep knocking on doors." This was January and we went back to see him in June. He said "Yes, there is something wrong."

We started to look more closely at the other stuff. Chris still could barely hold himself up on a push train. Chris was about two-and-a-half by this time. He was snuggly and affectionate. He loved to giggle and laugh. He was very passive and almost placid. He didn't cry a lot and I could always comfort him. I just thought I had an easy baby. He wasn't verbal at all. He had created his own sign language to interpret his world. We took him to church every Sunday and his sign for church was to pat the top of his head. That was what the pastor did on the way out of church. You had to figure out what the signs meant.

Different doctors. Different opinions

The pediatrician we were going to at the time had attributed a lot of his delays to the heart problem. We went to a different doctor to look at this further. He told us we needed to get Chris' hearing tested and find out why he was not talking. Everyone said we were older parents and we were doting on him, etc. Anyway, we did have the hearing test done and that was found to be fine. Then we took him to a center for developmental disabilities and had him tested there. They agreed that he was developmentally delayed and we should do some further medical testing to find out why. I guess to make sure it wasn't anything pathological.

At this point we went to a neurologist who said that it looked like cerebral palsy (CP), maybe. He said that it definitely wasn't anything that was regressive because he was improving. He really couldn't come up with anything specific so he labeled it "CP like syndrome." We really didn't want to do any invasive testing. He was only three years old.

School starts

We got him into a special school and they found him to be severely speech delayed and they started doing intensive speech therapy. He was getting speech, occupational therapy, and physical therapy very intensively in the classroom. That intervention really got him going. I am so grateful to this school. We still keep in touch with some of them. Anyway, Chris was talking by the fall after one summer program.

I remember after he started to talk, it struck me odd that he would always parrot me. Once he started to talk he was just totally verbal. It seemed that all his thoughts were gleaned from other people. It became obvious that he wasn't really initiating his own language. My radar went up. The other thing that I started to notice was that he didn't have a clue about reading other people's emotions. If I were furrowing my brow inquisitively he would think I was mad. He couldn't read normal expressions. In hindsight I can see a lot of that, but at the time I just thought that it was a little unusual.

More oddities emerge

Chris never had tantrums, and stuff that kids just seem to go through, he didn't seem to go through. We had a rectangular coffee table that he used to chew on. I did think that was an extreme kind of thing. Also, if you moved the table, he knew that it wasn't in the right place. Same thing in his room. He didn't want you to change anything because he needed it in order. He would cry and get angry. Change would set him off.

The other piece was that with other kids in the classroom Chris was always the observer, not a participant. He clung to any adult that was near by. He would watch the kids and seem interested. He didn't have a flat affect, but he never got in the fray. You could encourage him but it was always a struggle. You really had to push him. He would throw up, still does, if you force him to do something. From the anxiety I think. One time we went out to dinner and I left him with a sitter. She called us at the restaurant and said that Chris had thrown up. I said, "Is he breathing?" He was, "Did you clean it up?" She had. So what was the problem, I thought.

She probably thought that we were terrible but I wasn't going to freak out about this stuff. I thought it was just his anxiety. Then again, it was out of the realm of what I heard other moms talking about.

Vulnerability and obsessing

Chris does have an engaging way about him but it seems he has a huge sign on his chest that says, "I'm a victim." He's not picked on a lot but kids do seem to pick up on the vulnerability. He's learned enough about socialization now and he wants to be involved. If I have company he always comes down to talk, but it has to be what he wants to talk about.

Chris is obsessed with church. He knows the color of the vestments for the different seasons and can recite the liturgy. He volunteered over this past summer and the pastor thought it best if Chris wasn't there unless both the pastor and the secretary were present. I trust the pastor implicitly but these are the times we live in. This cut down on the time that Chris could be there. I told Chris this rule and he didn't like it. If you tell him a rule in black and white he gets it, but it's very hard to describe shades of gray. So then when he went back to school he wanted to know why he could be with other people there alone. What is good is that I'll explain something and he'll chew on it and I know I'll get more questions the next day. I've told him that sometimes people don't know the same rules, sometimes people choose to not follow the rule, and sometimes people bend it. We try to talk about what's fair. Like with the church pastor, he told him that he didn't like the rule and he didn't think it was fair but that he would follow it. He works it through and assimilates it. He really works on this social stuff. Sometimes to the point where I have to say, "Stop already!"

Perseveration

Chris will persist on some topics and I have to stop him or negotiate to talk about it again tomorrow for a certain amount of time. Like with church. He will talk about it for hours. He knew all the words to the entire mass by the age of three. He did a school project on the governing structure of the church. The interest can be a useful thing. When he was worrying about what he would do for the project I said, "Why don't you do something about the new bishop?" He didn't think they'd let him do that but they did. He did the whole nine yards to accomplish the project and even went in and made a speech.

Change

The hard part was to get him, in the beginning, to understand when things are different. When we went to a different church he just couldn't get why they weren't following the same rules. Chris notices everything. If something is off center or if the shape of something is different. He notices everything. He can pick up music very, very quickly. He can hear it once and know all the words. That is something I've tried to capitalize on. He's in chorus and the choir. He hears that tune and he's got it perfectly.

Regular school

When he finished his special school he went into a regular kindergarten. Again, he was always in the background. He was an observer. We joined the art museum and signed him up for art classes. We joined the zoo. We joined the science museum and signed him up for those classes. Getting him to participate in that stuff was very tough. And to prepare him to go was so hard. He would be so anxious the first day he would throw up. I tried to be gentle and calm him. I'd tell him it would be okay. Looking back on it now I see it wasn't quite right. At the time it was subtle stuff and we just thought he was kind of odd.

Fourth grade was a very difficult year. It was two classrooms put together with two teachers. There were 54 kids in one classroom. Chris had orthopedic surgery that year and he was in a wheelchair for 12 weeks. His father had surgery for cancer. Chris was not doing well academically and his male teacher was a threatener and a screamer. I can pretty much count on what Chris says because he remembers verbatim and he over interprets anger. He would come home and cry about stuff the teacher said. The other kids probably went home and forgot it. Chris spent the whole year with his hands folded thinking that if he did that it would be okay. His anxiety just escalated. Homework was a nightmare. Everything that you said to him was interpreted as highly critical. He was crying, not sleeping and he was bombing out academically. On top of that the other kids were maturing socially and he wasn't.

Socially, academically and emotionally he wasn't doing well. We had to schedule his surgery on break because he was so concerned about missing school. My thought process was that I didn't want to make him more anxious so even with surgery he never missed a day of school. It went okay because he wasn't in pain and he used a wheelchair.

The other woman teacher took my husband aside and said, "You might want to think about having Chris tested." She was concerned about the anxiety thing and didn't really know what was going on with him so she thought that it might be a good idea. This was the first time they approached us on the matter.

On friendship

I do want to comment on something else. We used to have Chris invite friends over to the house and they never reciprocated. Well, we were going to the mountains for vacation and we had Chris invite a friend. It was awful. Chris retreated. He wouldn't do anything. Wouldn't swim, go out in a boat, nothing. I think it was the change. I alternated between being affectionate and angry. I would tell him this was unacceptable behavior and he would say, "Okay Mom, I'll try." He put this phoney face on and I could tell he was struggling. I wanted him to knock it off. He had been so excited about the friend coming and talked and talked about it. On the car ride up they were okay. I don't know what it was, I can't even speculate but that first night he shut down. We probably should have sought counseling when we got back from the lake, but we didn't and he went right into that tough fourth-grade school year.

Concerns re-emerge

We attributed so much of it to his other medical problems. We did start putting these unusual behaviors together. We became more concerned particularly after the teacher approached my husband. This time we went to see a social work/counselor. We described what was going on and he said to get Chris out of the school setting. So we put him in a private school and decided to delay any testing until he was in the new school for a semester to see how much of what was going on was related to the environment he was in.

At the end of that first semester he was a lot calmer and less anxious. Those teachers approached us and said, "Let's test him just the same." So, he was tested that next winter. That testing came up with the diagnosis of a non-verbal learning disability. That was very, very vague. I had a friend who is a special educator and I showed her the report to help me interpret it. She agreed it was too vague and suggested another evaluation site. (The friend suggested a site that is familiar with autistic disorders, but Jan did not know that at the time.) We took him to yet another school and had him tested, again. During this time his anxiety was worsening. We reviewed all this stuff and three-quarters of the way through the conversation they said, "I think this is Asperger's syndrome." The evaluator never used the term autism. Now we could do something.

My quest all along has been to get this thing identified correctly and then to work with it. I'm not happy about the diagnosis. Do I wish he was normal? Yes! But reality is not going to go away. We actually were glad of the diagnosis and it made sense. Now we could do something about this.

After that we read and networked. We gathered all kinds of information. I'm not yet satisfied that he's had the best work-up that he could have had. I feel like I've been going by the seat of my pants. I took him for another evaluation with a school psychologist last summer and that report said pervasive developmental disorder, NOS (not otherwise specified) with an anxiety disorder.

Chris still prefers to not interact with his peers for the most part. He volunteers to clean the cafeteria and school rooms instead of going to the playground. He gravitates toward the odd kids. I was real concerned when my husband died because he didn't seem to have any emotional response to it. I don't know if he had a minimal response or if he has buried his feelings. It worries me.

The future and hope
I think about the future a lot. I get scared and depressed. I also remain hopeful. More than one person has said that he will be able to go to college. Society is more ready for different people. Is it going to be a struggle? Yes.

I know that he is here for a reason. I have a deep faith and trust in God. He will watch over Chris, He has this far! I also think that Chris can accomplish something significant. He has touched our lives in positive ways. He is a wonderful person!

Lynn

Lynn is a little girl we met a few years ago. Over these few years she has made wonderful progress and is such a happy child. Like others, though she struggles with social difficulties, her uniqueness is a special gift. Lynn's mother, Cynthia, is yet another example of a parent's love put into action! This is their story.

"Such a happy baby!"
As an infant, Lynn was such a happy baby. A delightful child! She smiled and laughed, and she slept! I loved that, sleep. I have an older child and he didn't sleep so I loved that. She was a doll. We moved up here when she was about 13 months,

and she had walked by her first birthday, she had a few words and was putting a few words together. At that point I was more concerned about getting my almost three-year-old into kindergarten school. Then I had more time with Lynn and by 20 months of age, I was beginning to get concerned. Her language had stopped. I didn't understand why she could sit and look at a video forever and why she wasn't interested in books. She didn't want to be read to. She would only let some people hold her and she wouldn't call me "Mommy." She really liked her Dad, and called him by name. They were very close. And, she liked her brother and called him by name. But she wouldn't call me by name. Looking back on it now, I think that I was just an extension of her.

"Then tantrums, as if you were sticking pins in her"

She didn't really lose her language and she could use words to get her needs met, but it didn't progress. She got stuck in time. And then she started to tantrum. Then came big tantrums. I tried to make her talk, thinking that if I don't get it for her she'll have to use words. "Tell me this?" or "Tell me you want juice?" She would just lose it totally. Throw herself on the floor. It would escalate as if you were sticking pins in her. Of course, I was concerned about her so I went to my pediatrician. I was a "crazy woman" and was told to stop reading medical books. I would say to the doctor, "Why is she doing this or that?" "There's something wrong, there's something wrong." And he said, "Stop comparing her to other children. She's a typical second child." "Her brother is very talkative and she can't get a word in edgewise. Look how happy she is playing with her toy."

Again, when I think back, she played with only one toy and it had to be a certain way. After talking to the doctor I thought that maybe I was wrong. I thought, "Well, we'll see." As a mother you just get that feeling. Anyway, the doctor said to get Lynn playing with more kids.

At that time a new school was opening near by and I thought that would be perfect. I had her around kids. She had played with more kids than her brother had ever played with at that age. But I thought maybe she needed more time with kids. She's a different child. She was just about 28 months old at this time. She went to this program once a week and I expressed to the teacher my concerns about Lynn's language, and again, she told me that each child is different. The teacher said she would keep an eye on it.

"No! There is something wrong"

By the end of the year, she had made some progress but it was very slow. Not just in language but other areas, as well. Anything that had to do with music, she led the group. She loved the group setting only if it had to do with music time. Otherwise, she had nothing to do with the other children. I thought that she just preferred to play by herself but by the time she turned three I thought, "No, there is something really wrong." I went back to the pediatrician and told her that Lynn was putting words together and had been for a year but that she hadn't gone any further. And she was having trouble socializing. How was she going to learn to socialize if she couldn't talk? The doctor thought that maybe something was a little off, but still wasn't too concerned.

"She's not THAT!"

Certainly I wasn't thinking it was autism! In school I had only learned of the most severe. I had a family member who worked at a residence for disabled people and I would help out in the summer. The disabilities were so severe. The autistic people I saw would wander around and bang their heads, make weird noices, sit in the most bizarre pretzel positions, and they looked distorted. To me that was autism. I thought of Lynn, and I thought, "She's not that!" She's a smart kid and there has to be a way to fix that little glitch. Then everything will be okay.

"I was going to fix her"

I was with her day in and day out. But I did think that during the summer, when her brother was at camp, I would have time with just her and I was going to fix this thing. I was going to get her potty trained and I was going to fix her.

That summer she did do well, as long as we were doing what she wanted to do she was wonderful. She started to name things and was happy to see me. Before that, I wasn't Daddy so it didn't matter if I came in a room. She progressed. That's why I didn't do something sooner because every time I got really crazy with worry she would do something new and I would say to myself, "Stop! You're making yourself crazy!"

A girlfriend came to visit after that. When we picked her up Lynn didn't look at her. She said, "Why isn't she looking at me?" and I said, "She's looking at your hat." The friend replied, "But why isn't she looking at my face?" "So she doesn't like your face, don't take it personally!" I said, "She's just a different child."

I was angry but I'm grateful that she said something. She had the courage to say something that other people had thought but hadn't said. My brother who had worked with developmentally disabled kids hadn't said anything. He thought it was something, but he didn't think it was autism.

Evaluation

The pediatrician had said that because I was so worried about this thing he would refer me to a speech therapist. It took us six weeks to get to see her and it was a terrible visit. Now that I know autism, Lynn had all the earmark signs: inattentiveness, lack of eye contact, all the language stuff. I mean this is a professional and all she said was, "I can't test her, she's too uncooperative. She needs to be disciplined." She started to tell me how to raise my child. I looked at that. I wasn't pleased with her but I did think about what she said. I had another child who was perfectly fine so it couldn't be my parenting. As we went to leave Lynn said, "Put your coat on Daddy, let's go!" She had never put a sentence together like that before. I thought, "whoa!" We left with mixed emotions.

I was committed to spending more time here. I was going to make the difference.

I don't understand why she (the evaluator) couldn't have said, "Maybe there's something going on here." Or, "You should have her looked at further." "I'm having a hard time testing her, but maybe you should go elsewhere." She was a professional after all.

Our extended family lives a few hours away so we don't see them a whole lot. One time we left the children for a weekend with family and I was so scared about doing it. But my parents said, "Oh, she'll be fine, don't worry!" After the weekend they said, "She listened for us." And, I thought, "Did you feed her all day?" That's my mother's thing. My mother said, "There's nothing wrong with her. She eats!" Lynn connects with her grandfather very well. She seems to love men. So, anyway, the grandparents thought things were fine.

On the home front

Meanwhile, I was trying to keep clothes on her and go shopping. She was awful in the store and she had started this habit of getting up at three o'clock in the morning and taking her clothes off in front of our mirror. Then she would do a Mickey Mouse routine. Every night. It was getting harder and harder. Then again, when I was doing something that she wanted to do she was an absolute delight. I started trying to slip in little stuff that I wanted to do. I finally got her potty trained. It took a week but I did it. Still couldn't get her to read. Except for this one book, *Goodnight Moon*! We had to read it the same way and touched the same pictures. I had to even use the same voice. If I tried to change anything she would have a fit. Or, if I would try to slip in a new book she would say, "No!" She still wasn't saying "Mommy" and she referred to herself as "Lynn" but wouldn't say "me" or "I." She didn't use pronouns correctly.

"The Miracle Worker"

My husband was still thinking that she was progressing and just needed a little help. By this point I was thinking, "You come live in my shoes all day long with this." This is the weirdest thing, but I had this experience one day when I had a flash of "The Miracle Worker", the story of Helen Keller with Patty Duke and Ann Bancroft, and I thought, "I'm like Ann Bancroft. There's something really wrong here!" I told myself, "No, no, no. You're such a drama queen. Get this out of your mind." But there was that flash.

The summer continued. Lynn was supposed to start kindergarten school in the fall and I couldn't sleep at night. I would replay the whole day in my head and then wake up my husband. He finally agreed to get more evaluation, I think so that he could get some sleep. I told him, "If they tell me I'm crazy, that'll be great!" My insides were telling me something was not right and during the day I could work it out of my mind but at night it was keeping me up. Between that and the nightly visits of Mickey Mouse, I couldn't think straight.

Developmental pediatrician

I called my brother and told him I was terribly worried about Lynn. That's the first time he said to me that he thought there was something wrong. He told me to go to the school district. I didn't want to go to the school so he told me to go to a developmental pediatrician. He told me he knew of one in our area because he had looked around. I wanted to know why he didn't say anything to me sooner. He said, "Because you didn't ask me." If he had told me it may have given me a little push that I needed. I think people just thought that she was spoiled rotten. People aren't accepting of a disability when it isn't visible. Here was this beautiful child, with awful behavior. People don't jump to conclusions about the parents when they see a child who looks different. They think there's something wrong with the child, not the parent.

I called to get an appointment with the developmental pediatrician and I told them my concerns on the phone. I asked them if they thought that we needed to come in and they said yes. They had a cancellation the next day and we took the opening.

"Everything stopped"

During the evaluation she did all her little tricks. I still thought it was a little thing. I never realized it was going to be serious. The minute the doctor said the "A" word (autism), I shut down. I couldn't hear. I thought everything just stopped. I was watching the doctor's mouth move and I knew I needed to listen to this but I just couldn't. Later on I wondered if that is what it's like for Lynn. To be detached in that way. I had never had that kind of experience before. I asked if I could come back with my husband and we arranged for that. I took home information, but I left out of it. On the way home I thought, "I have to call, I have to call." So I pulled off the road, got Lynn out of the car and called my husband from one of those phones on the side of the highway. He said, "So, what did they think?" I told him they said Lynn was autistic. He asked if I was okay and I said, "No, I'm really not."

No matter what was going on, we knew Lynn had deficits and we had to get her help. In one sense I thought, "Okay, I'm not crazy," and now we have a name for this. I hadn't thought about autism but my gut had been telling me for a while that things weren't right. We returned to the developmental pediatrician for more discussion and we did some reading about the disorder. We did begin to see how Lynn fit the diagnosis and my husband wanted to investigate further. I wanted to get help for Lynn started.

Shortly after that, I got very angry at all those people who could have identified this sooner. I learned about "the window of time" (idea that there is a specific period of time when a child is most responsive to intervention) and I felt we had lost time. The doctor was very clear though, and I don't think that they all are, of what we had to do from there. That was helpful. The doctor didn't throw her arms up and tell us to go start checking out institutions. She did say that Lynn was going to need one-on-one supervision and intervention focused on her particular areas of need. She told us that we as parents were going to have to be very involved and follow through on all her training. She told us that there were a lot of good programs out there and that we were going to have to find a program that would work for us. We got the wheels in motion after that visit.

I do remember when it all started to sink in. We were in the car driving and the kids were sleeping. I heard these awful noises and realized that they were coming from me. And, I couldn't stop. I just sobbed. I had the ability though to say, "I can't do this right now. I have to do this."

Finding intervention

When I was looking into approaches I just felt that ABA (applied behavioral analysis) was the only one that really had success with children like Lynn. I couldn't understand how play therapy was going to be different than what I was already doing. She really needed structure and she is in her own little world. I felt that play therapy was going to let her stay in that own little world and not pull her into ours. It went back to making the parents the bad guys because we must not have been playing right if they were going to play differently to help her. This is a neurological disorder and it has to be treated like one.

I called another program and they worked with a lot of disabled kids. They said Lynn would be a good role model for their other students. I wanted Lynn to have good role models, not to be one.

The program that we did find was very upbeat and optimistic. I thought this was totally nuts, or this was exactly what we needed. I went to see the program. It was hard. The smell was of antiseptic. The whole thing was hard. I looked in the room and it was cheerful. The director took me in a room and asked me to point out which child I thought was autistic. I couldn't guess. I watched this little boy playing, sharing, talking. He was diagnosed autistic six months before. I said, "Okay. When can we start?"

From there I had to go to the school district. I think I threw myself on the chairman's floor! I cried. I let it go. I said,

"You have to help me!" Until the age of six, the brain is so incredible. You have to make the difference when the brain can best accommodate. Maybe there are pockets there that we can tap into or circuits that haven't been stimulated. It made sense to me to do a lot during this time and I wanted the school district to agree. I'd do anything to help my kid. The school district agreed to sending Lynn to the program.

We learned the ABA techniques used in the school and did a great deal at home as well. We included activities, such as swimming, into our family life. It was important to us to have a family life as well as spend a good deal of time on training skills for Lynn. It was hard to find time for it all.

We were also concerned about how Lynn's brother was handling all this. After all, this was his sister. At this point she wasn't invading his territory or his toys. I asked another mother how she had explained this to her other children and she told me that she described it to the children as being like having a monster in your head. And, I asked him to help me get rid of that monster. I said to him, "You know how we have to leave places sometimes because Lynn can't behave, or you can't come in my bed because it would be too upsetting to Lynn. Well, there's an awful monster in Lynn's head and it affects her brain. What we have to do is get that monster smaller. It's not your sister. It's the monster. She doesn't want that monster in her brain." It seemed to really make sense to him and I found that when she would do something awful, he would say, "That monster is doing bad things. I don't like that monster." He asked me how we were going to get rid of the monster. I told him we had to teach her and her good brain cells would get bigger. Later he was sitting with her pointing to a book saying, "Lynn, this is an apple." Lynn adores her brother. Sometimes he still says, "Mommy, it's just not fair." I say, "You're right. It's just not fair."

Things can get rough. We have moments. She'll want to wear shorts and a T-shirt and it's snowing outside. She's in a fit while her brother is trying to have breakfast and get the school bus. Fortunately, I have a half hour after she leaves to spend a little time with him. It's tough.

"You have to be an advocate"

Lynn went into a regular kindergarten after two years of special programming. She had the support of an aide, a speech therapist and occupational therapist. The previously used ABA techniques were carried over to the school program. It's your child and above all you know your child better than anybody else. You have to be a major advocate for her. I've always felt that it was my responsibility to raise the child and the teachers are there to help me. They are there to work with me and help to create a fine human being. I've had to keep a close eye on things or things would get shifted around. When they said that they didn't have enough speech therapists I told them to hire another one.

"I want her to be okay"

I just wish I knew how Lynn is feeling because she can't tell me. I hope there is a day that she will be able to tell me how she was feeling at certain times. As her mother, I want to make her feel better. I want her to be okay.

Luke

Ellen stood at the doorway. Her initial greeting was proceeded by an exhaustive sigh. Introductions were made and her tension visibly cleared as she settled on the coach beside a tray of tea. We began the interview after an informal chat. Ellen had a great desire to share the story of her four-year-old son, Luke. It was apparent that this woman had a very "full plate" yet it was important to her to take time to share her story. And, share she did.

"The bottom fell out that year!"

Between September and October, as Luke approached his second birthday, he developed a series of ear infections that lasted for a year. With the ear infections came a total loss of language. Before that time he had words. He became progressively more irritable and weepy, and it seemed his behavior worsened when he was on antibiotics. And, he was on antibiotics from October to May. He lost skills and knowledge that I knew he had. He was still able to do simple puzzles and was particularly adept at shape sorting. Up until that point he was a very cheerful, happy child. At least that is what I perceived. The bottom fell out that year!

Once the ear infections had cleared up and Luke was off antibiotics, he was not the same child. We noticed that he spaced out a lot, would not stay on task, especially on table top activities. He wouldn't be able to do even simple things like painting. He started to do bizarre things like trying to eat the paint or run the paint brushes through his hair. All he wanted to do was sit in the corner with his car and spin the wheels.

When he stopped responding to his name being called we thought that he had a hearing problem. We were assured by his doctor and family members that he'd be better. Blah, blah, blah! I was concerned about the loss of language and I was told that he was jealous of other kids in the daycare I had started in my home. Luke started talking around the time he was one. Maybe he had about 20 words, but then he just stopped using them. He would shriek to communicate what he wanted.

"There we were, supporting each other's denial"

Looking back on it now, I can see that there were peculiarities even in infancy. Even at one month. I breast fed, and I noticed that he preferred to look at the wall instead of me. I had read about that being a sign of early autism. Ironically, my husband came home one day when I was crying and I told him of my concern about this. He said, "Oh, that's okay. One of our neighbors was saying exactly the same thing." At the time those were reassuring words. Well, the neighbor's child is now diagnosed with Asperger's. There we were supporting each other's denial. Our children were doing the same things.

Luke was extraordinarily sensitive to sound. He could not tolerate a lullaby. I had to sing him Beatles songs to sooth him, but lullabies, like "Twinkle, Twinkle, Little Star" and "Mary had a Little Lamb" would send him from the room crying hysterically. We just figured he was sensitive. He did like people. He cuddled. It was just his eye contact was poor and he was hearing sensitive. Now, we were a new mom and dad, and we didn't know what any of this meant. We knew that he liked to cuddle with us, and his grandparents.

Then I started taking other kids in for daycare and he didn't seem to like them. He liked older children but not his peers. He followed the older kids around and would inappropriately grab on to them. Even that degree of socialization decreased over time.

"I was not a good mother"

Luke was having problems because I was not a good mother. That was a pretty universal opinion of friends and family. I was pushing him too hard. I wasn't pushing him hard enough. Some family members said it was because I was playing Disney movies and the violence in them was what was disturbing him. So I was supposed to believe that it was because he watched "Beauty and the Beast" that he had behavior problems. That's why he wouldn't sit down or paint? That was the reason he just ran around without direction, because he was disturbed from the movie?

Others suggested that it was something in his diet so I took just about everything out of his diet. Then it was just that I worry too much, or that I was too nervous. I had some serious moments of insecurity.

Once Luke got the diagnosis it seemed to immediately lift some weighted burden that rested on my shoulders. Everybody got off my back. I think my husband apologized on behalf of his family for their notion that I was too nervous and I was damaging Luke. They all have come to realize now that I had extraordinary demands on me.

By this point I had a colicky infant, Luke's new brother, and Luke with his difficulties. I recall that every day was utter hell for me. There was great satisfaction in saying, and knowing, "It's not because of me!"

Who initially became concerned?

I was the one most concerned initially and my mother after that. My husband had some concerns but he thought that Luke would outgrow them. The pediatrician was also very concerned. On Luke's second birthday, when I told her that Luke had lost language, the doctor referred us to the county for early intervention. That was, as I explained before, at a point at which I wasn't ready to accept anything serious was wrong.

After he was evaluated at 25 months of age, the evaluators said that he was functioning at about the 11-month level. I knew innately that my kid had a lot of smarts. I guess my denial kicked in and I assured myself that he was not that bad. I didn't understand. They were very nice and all, but I didn't think that they took into account that a child can vary from day to day and that they weren't able to get him to do things that I had been able to get him to do to that previous summer. I didn't realize what we were looking at and that the loss of those skills was highly significant. Nobody spelled that out to me.

The evaluators wanted to do more testing. I told them that I thought it was a speech problem and that I really didn't think I wanted to do anything yet, in terms of initiating intervention services. They asked if they could come back in six months. I remember the two examiners looking at each other. I didn't understand the significance of those glances. Now I do.

The examiners called six months later and wanted to come see him again. I was in a full-blown depression by then brought on by the stresses of taking care of Luke, taking care of other kids, and the criticism from others. It was not appropriate that I didn't respond to the phone messages, or follow up on getting more testing. It was just that I did not want to hear one other person call me a lousy mother.

"It's not you! It's your child!"

A few months after that I went to a birthday party. I was speaking to the mother of the child who was having the party. She was watching Luke and she was watching me. Finally she approached me and asked, "How are things going with Luke?" We began to talk and I started to share everything. She said, "You know I'm a single mother with two girls and I don't work as hard as you are on your one boy." She was being very sweet. "Does your pediatrician know?" I continued to tell her the whole story. She encouraged me to call my pediatrician again. "Ellen, it's not you! It's your child! You didn't do anything wrong."

Some time after that encounter, I found out that the woman at the party worked with disabled people and knew about autism. She knew the signs and she had been so sweet to me. She approached me and she did it the right way. She said, "It's not you!" I bless her. She was the first voice that was not critical.

The waiting game

Then it was the waiting game. I didn't realize I could have had him seen through urgent visit but instead we waited two months for the next available appointment with the pediatrician. I explained everything to him. He was astonished that Luke was not getting services. "Did you call the county? You've got to call the county right away!"

I called the county when he was almost 35 months. They informed me that they couldn't get out to see Luke until after his third birthday and that meant that we had to call the local school district to get Luke evaluated again. The local school district couldn't get out until after the holidays. From August until January it was just the waiting game.

"Don't you think he's odd?"

The person from the preschool finally came. It turned out to be the same psychologist who had evaluated Luke before. When she saw Luke she looked shocked. Her mouth dropped open. It was January and Luke was lying down on the wet pavement running his cars back and forth. His shirt had rolled up so his belly was flat against the cold pavement. When I had tried to get him up, he had screamed so I just let him be. She said, "Don't you think he's odd?" and I said, "Yes." (A simple answer that had been long in coming.) "I'm so glad that you're telling me this because I've been thinking he was odd all year and everyone told me he was just being a kid," I said. I was so glad she agreed that it was odd because I felt like I was living in this unreality.

Eventually we got Luke inside and attempted to continue on with further evaluation. The psychologist watched Luke as he ate some cereal. He was shoveling it into his mouth with his hands. "Does he do this all the time?" she asked. I said, "Yes, but I've been told not to pressure him to use a spoon." I think she had to make sure that I wasn't a negligent mother. I needed to hear that I wasn't an over-worrying mother.

At that time, the psychologist was very concerned, very sweet and very sympathetic to me. When she was leaving she said, "He definitely qualifies for special preschool and I want to put him in for more evaluation." I asked her what she thought he had. She responded, "I don't know. I'm not a medical doctor. It may be PDD." I asked her what that was and when she said that it was on the autistic spectrum, I could have thrown up! "Don't tell me that!" was all I could say.

The word AUTISM

When I thought of autism all that came to mind were kids banging their heads against the wall. This psychologist was the first one to use that word, AUTISM! When I look back on it, I wish that the word had been used earlier because it put the fear of God in me. Maybe every parent is different but because people (referring to professionals) were busy trying to protect my feelings what they really did was delay Luke from getting services. I hadn't realized the importance of getting him services right away. Nobody told me of the significance of lost skills and that is very important. I think that people were putting the focus on me, and my mothering, and not on Luke.

Luke was approved for services through the school district and he entered school in March.

"It can't be! He loves his cat!"

We went to see a developmental pediatrician. That was terrible. We were just put off by her manner. She was very harsh and went straight to the point without giving us enough background. She didn't acknowledge any of his skills and she made it a very black and white issue. This doctor did not look at this as a spectrum disorder and felt that our son was not even playing like a one-year-old. One productive thing did come from the visit though, and that is that she directed us to ABA (applied behavioral analysis). It was a little scary that this doctor thought that this was the only method that would give our son a chance at recovery. She did say that he was not retarded but that he was very socially and verbally impaired and in need of a lot of help. This visit had a big impact on us and we didn't waste any time in getting him into a program from that point, however, we still weren't really accepting of the diagnosis because it wasn't presented as a disorder of varying degrees. Luke didn't fit their image of what it meant to be autistic. Luke was not aloof and he liked to be touched. When he wanted to be left alone we thought it was because demands were being made of him and that he was extremely stubborn. He certainly did things on his own terms! Luke loves his family and grandparents. When he sees his grandfather's car he runs out to it. On the basis of those things, I rejected the diagnosis. He even loves his cat!

"She wore on us like water on a stone"

We had to wait until May for another opinion. Between March and May Luke started to do some bizarre behaviors. He started walking on tip toes, arching his back, and had weird posturing and facial expressions He also started to bang his head. By the time we went in May, I was getting an average of two to three hours of sleep a night and was severely sleep deprived. I didn't want to even drive the car.

Besides watching the changes in Luke's behavior, the family social worker at the school wore on us like water on a stone to get us to accept the diagnosis. Luke wasn't progressing and was actually regressing. He needed to go into one-on-one therapy and needed the diagnosis or he wasn't able to get that. His therapists were using ABA techniques and they felt he needed more. But we had to accept it first. The family therapist kept calling and kept repeating what she was observing. In May, she started explaining the options for servicing and by the time we went to the second opinion visit, we had accepted the need for the diagnosis.

Luke was higher functioning during the second exam. This doctor is the one who laid it out as a spectrum. The doctor emphasized Luke's loss of skills. He really discussed his play and how he was occupied only for a little while, and that it doesn't progress. He goes on to something else too quickly. Kids over three won't just drop something. The imagination world kicks in and they go into their own fantasy world. This doctor's approach was easier to take. And, we were more ready for the information

Coping with "A whole new world"!

I, to be perfectly honest, have been seriously depressed since Luke's birth. There have been periods of elevation. At times my depression was replaced with trying to learn as much as I could. I was driven by a lot of anger at that point. The depression lifted for a couple of months then it settled back in heavily until recently.

When I was younger I had trouble with depression. It is in my family. This is a personal point of mine. In the literature a lot of people will say, in a detached way, that autism correlates heavily with a family history of depression and other conditions like obsessive compulsive disorder (OCD). But then when you're actually working with the professionals, it doesn't seem to be a recognized factor and it's not discussed. They aren't recognizing that parents themselves might be suffering from some of these things and it's going to have an impact on how they handle this. In my own work I always followed the idea that you "mother the mother" so that she can be a good mother. I think that when one is dealing with parents who may be carrying some of these traits (such as depression or OCD) this needs to be taken into account. All this information is coming at you, like how to teach him to potty train, and every little step you're going to follow, and how you're going to reinforce him. Meantime, you've got a whole package inside you. All these intense emotions inside you and you have to learn this whole new way of teaching, this whole new way of parenting, this whole new way of living, this whole new way of structuring your life.

I eventually sought professional help. She tried medications but found them too energy zapping at a time when my child was particularly physically demanding. I could not afford to lose energy. Now I deal with it by talking to other parents. It's really important to know that it didn't just happen to you. It happens to a lot of people. Also, I realized that I needed to take care of myself. I was totally spent. Now, I try to take selfish advantage of any time to myself. I blast music loud and sing. I also do solitary stuff quietly because I have to talk and talk to my son. I garden, read, quiet things.

The emotions are so powerful! I tried to get back in touch with my religious upbringing and make some peace with God as I picture him. I see my child as a sick child. I see my child as a child who has brain damage. He can recover from it by tapping in to other areas of the brain that aren't damaged. Any time that a parent has a sick child, or a hurt child, the emotions are very powerful. If you've been battling depression your whole life and you choose to have a child it is an act of faith. You say I'm going to take this chance. I'm going to prove that life is worth living and then this is done to you. That's how you feel. That it hasn't just been done to your child, it's been done to you. And, you knew all along that God didn't love you. That's how I felt. How can a merciful God do this to this little child? In the meantime, everyone around you is talking very rationally about what to do and you're just swirling with emotions. You have to package the emotions and put them to the side so that you can do what needs to be done for the child. The time is about them, not you. But the suffering is very real. The depression is very real. A professional could help in the healing process by acknowledging this.

The spouse

My husband and my own defenses went down at the same time. We've been fortunate in that we were in the same place at the same time and agreed on what to do. Otherwise, it would have been hellish. I'm the one who is at home doing the teaching and my husband realizes this. He recognizes that Luke does as well as I'm doing. The sleep deprivation has been hard. My husband will do extra housework. He's been supportive. We also have respite and that's good. His parents baby-sit sometimes. Luke's whole life is behavioral intervention so it's hard for someone else to care for him. It's all directed activity or drills. Our whole life is around that. Luke has made a lot of progress so it's been worth every minute of it. We've gone from a child who was head banging to one who is verbal.

"He's like a little boy!"

Luke now asks all sort of questions. He has better associations. He saw the snow blower and said, "Snow comes soon. Then it's Christmas." He's starting to learn more easily and he's generalizing information. His language is just starting to have melody. It's not just flat. Intonation is lovely. It's worth it. It's a hell of a way to live, but it's worth it. He's more like a little boy.

"He enters our world!"

I want him to stop being autistic. The first year sometimes I'd take him to his room and then collapse in the middle of the living room floor because I was so totally exhausted and overwhelmed. Feeling alone, so angry. We're trying to make our children like other human beings. I want my son to listen to the songs I love and get up to dance. That has been part of my own behavioral therapy, to show him dancing. My husband loves to ski so we're teaching him to ski. It thrilled us when he saw the snow and said he wanted to ski. This is our reinforcement. When our child enters our world.

Diet

I believe that these children are physically compromised in ways that we do not yet understand. I believe in a special diet for my particular child. At first it didn't seem that the diet was working and he actually had worsened tantrums. Then miraculously his speech just took off.

Every component helps a little bit and when orchestrated together we saw a big change. We see his diet and treatments as supportive of his intervention but not in place of intervention. His ABA is critical for him.

How do you feel about his progress?

There are times I don't know where we are. There are so many areas of concern and it's hard to keep focused on those. Then out of the blue self-stimulating behaviors keep coming back. They increase, they decrease. You talk about the spectrum disorder and some days they fall here, some days there. Overall I know he's made good progress. As parents, what we need is the input from the professionals to help us keep a reality check. We're too close to it every day

Looking to the future

I try not to think long term, because it scares the dickens out of me. I think about today and tomorrow and maybe next year. I don't think any further than that because I don't know what we'll be looking at. I know what we're hoping for. I hope we're looking at college. It's like a tightrope and I just have to focus on the next step. I've got to focus on what we've got to do today.

I think about the future and I pray. The "faith factor" is the only thing that keeps my sanity because if I kept hating God I would not have been able to function. I need to believe that there is a higher plan. I need to believe that we're being tested to see exactly what we're made of and I can't ask why God did this to this little child. I need to think that Luke was a soul that was to exist here. There are trials of misfortune and trials of fortune through Luke. We all carry burdens. It's how we carry them that matters.

"Faith factor"

You have to decide which side you're on when times are hard. You have hard decisions to make. There are a lot of personal dreams and wants that you could be pursuing right now, and society would not be judging you too hard. I've had to ask, "What is the right thing to do?" I didn't agonize over my decision. To stay with him was the only decision because it was the right one. I could be working outside the home and making a lot more money but who would do what I do for Luke. I mean, yes, I want to go swimming, and I want to go to lunch. But, not if it's at a cost to Luke.

When Luke was first diagnosed I felt rage at God inside. It was an act of faith for me to have a baby and I felt let down. I thought I want nothing to do with a God that lets these things happen to children. The only way I could deal with it was to think that this soul of Luke made a choice to be here. All I can figure is that we have lessons to learn from him and through him. It's not that my husband and I are are bad people and therefore need to be tested. We are all tested. It's just that we are being tested in a very overt way. People who have great fortunes are tested by people who are less fortunate. Their tests may be harder because it's so easy to ignore. Maybe we're actually fortunate because our tests are overt and the answers more clear cut. For example, if I had typical children maybe I'd be working full time and not spending the time with them. I might miss their childhood in the flurry of day to day, as I see happening in some families. I mean their kids are okay, maybe they are growing up a little too fast though. I don't regret my choice to be with my child at all.

"I wish I had followed my instincts!"

Looking back I wish I had been more attentive at the first evaluation. I wish I had followed my instincts and gotten early intervention sooner. That I feel pretty guilty about that. But since we accepted the diagnosis I think we've made good decisions for Luke

Final comments

Programs are individualized and what works for one child might not work for another. This is super important. If a parent hears from other parents that they did something with their child, parents need to go back to their therapists and talk about the idea and possibility of working that into the child's plan. I think it's great to go on line, talk to other parents. But you have to look at the information critically for the individual child. Parents need to look to the specialists for support and work together. The kids need to learn how to "be"!

Resources

Books for general review

Since the initial writing of this book many good resources have become available. We offer here a small sampling but encourage readers to seek further information to meet their specific areas of concern and need.

Attwood, T. (1998) *Asperger's Syndrome*. London: Jessica Kingsley Publishers.

Attwood, T. (2007) *The Complete Guide to Asperger's Syndrome*. London: Jessica Kingsley Publishers.

Frith, U. (1991) *Autism and Asperger Syndrome*. Cambridge: Cambridge University Press.

Frith, U. (2008) *Autism: A Very Short Introduction*. Oxford: Oxford University Press.

Koegal, L. and LaZebnick, C. (2004) *Overcoming Autism*. New York, NY: Viking.

Seigal, B. (1996) *The World of the Autistic Child*. Oxford: Oxford University Press.

Volkmer, F.R., Cohen, D.J. and Klin, A. (2005) *Handbook of Autism and Pervasive Developmental Disorders*. Chichester: John Wiley.

Wetherby, A.M. and Prizant, B.M. (2001) *Autism Spectrum Disorders, A Transactional Developmental Perspective*. Baltimore, MD: Brookes Publishing.

Helpful resource books

Dunn, K. and Curtis, M. (2003) *The Incredible 5-Point Scale*. Overland Park, KS: Autism Asperger Publishing Co.

Frost, L.A. and Bondy, A.S. (1994) *The Picture Exchange Communication System*. Cherry Hill, NJ: Pyramid Educational Consultants, Inc.

Grandin, T. (2006) *Thinking in Pictures*, Expanded Edition. New York, NY: Random House.

Gray, C. (2010) *The New Social Story Book*. Arlington, TX: Future Horizons.

Gray, C. (1994) *Comic Strip Conversation*. Arlington, TX: Future Horizons.

Greene, R. (2005) *The Explosive Child: A New Approach for Understanding and Parenting Easily Frustrated Chronically Inflexible Children*. New York, NY: Harper Collins Publishers.

Greenspan, S. (2006) *Engaging Autism: Helping Children Relate, Communicate and Think with DIR Floortime Approach.* Cambridge, MA: DaCapo Press.

Greenspan, S., Simons, R. and Weider, S. (1998) *The Child with Special Needs: Encouraging Intellectual and Emotional Growth.* Cambridge, MA: DaCapo Press.

Gutstein, S.E. and Sheely, R. (2002) *Relationship Development with Young Children; Social and Emotional Activities for Asperger Syndrome, Autism, PDD, and NLD.* London: Jessica Kingsley Publishers.

Gutstein, S.E. (2000) *Autism Aspergers: Solving the Relationship Puzzle – A New Developmental Program that Opens the Door to Lifelong Social and Emotional Growth.* London: Jessica Kingsley Publishers.

Harris, S.L. and Weiss, M.J. (2006) *Right From the Start: Behavioral Intervention for Young Children with Autism, A Guide for Parents and Professionals.* Bethesda, MD: Woodbine House.

Koegel, R.L. and Koegel, L.K. (1995) *Teaching Children with Autism: Strategies for Initiating Positive Interaction and Improving Learning Opportunities.* Baltimore, MD: Brookes Publishing.

McAfee, J. (2002) *Navigating The Social World: A Curriculum for Individuals with Aspergers, High-functioning Autism and Related Disorders.* Arlington, TX: Future Horizons.

Myles, B.S., Trautman, M.L. and Schelvan, R.L. (2004) *The Hidden Curriculum: Practical Solutions for Understanding Rules in Social Situations.* Overland Park, KS: Autism Asperger Publishing Co.

National Autism Center (2009) *National Standards Project – Addressing the Need for Evidence-based Practice Guidelines for Autism Spectrum Disorders.* Randolph, MA: National Autism Center.

National Research Council (2001) *Educating Children with Autism.* Committee on Educational Interventions for Children with Autism, Division of Behavioral and Social Sciences and Education. Washington DC: National Academy Press.

Ozonoff, S., Dawson, G. and McPartland, J. (2002) *A Parent's Guide to Asperger syndrome and High Functioning Autism: How to Meet the Challenges and Help our Child Thrive.* New York: Guilford Press.

Publishers with focus on autistic spectrum disorders and surrounding issues

Autism Asperger Publishing Co. (Overland Park, KS, USA)

Brookes Publishing Co. (Baltimore, MD, USA)

Future Horizons (Arlington, TX, USA)

Guilford Press (New York, USA)

Jessica Kingsley Publishers (London, UK)

Woodbine House (Bethesda, MD, USA)

Research-based journals

There are many additional journals from organizations that are helpful for parents.

Autism: The International Journal of Research and Practice

Behavioral Intervention

Education and Training in Developmental Disabilities

Exceptional Children

Focus on Autism and Other Developmental Disorders

Journal of ABA

Journal of Autism and Developmental Disorders

Journal of Early Intervention

Journal of Positive Behavior Support

Websites

www.asperger.net

www.asperger.org

www.autism.about.com

www.autism-pdd.net

www.autismresearch.org

www.autism-resources.com

www.autism-society.org

www.autismspeaks.org

www.futurehorizons-autism.com

www.jeaniemcafee.com

www.info@nationalautismcenter.org

www.childstudycenter.yale.edu/clinics/

www.nationalautismassociation.org

www.nih.gov

www.nimh.nih.gov

www.rdiconnect.com

www.thegraycenter.org

www.udel.edu/bkirby/asperger

www.teacch.com/

References

American Psychiatric Association (APA) (1994) *Diagnostic and Statistical manual of Mental Disorders*, 4th edn. Washington, DC: American Psychiatric Association.

Frith, U. (ed.) (1991) *Autism and Asperger syndrome.* Cambridge: Cambridge University Press.

Frost, L. and Bondy, A. (1994) *The Picture Exchange Communication System, Training Manual.* Cherry Hill, NJ: Pyramid Educational Consultants, Inc.

Greenspan, S. and Wieder, S. (1998) *The Child with Special Needs.* Reading, MA: Addison-Wesley.

Lewine, J.D., Andrew, R., Chez, M., Patil, A., *et al.* (1999). Magnetoencephalographic patterns of epileptiform activity in children with regressive autism spectrum disorders. *Pediatrics 104*, 405–418.

Maurice, C., Green, G. and Luce, S. (1996) *Behavioral Intervention for Young Children with Autism.* Austin, TX: Pro-Ed, Inc.

Mesibov, G.B. (1994) A comprehensive program for serving people with autism and their families: The TEACCH model. In J.L. Matson (ed.) *Autism in Children and Adults: Etiology, Assessment, and Intervention.* (pp.85–97). Belmont, CA: Brooks & Cole

About the Authors

Barbara L. Quinn brings to her writing over 25 years of nursing experience. In her role as Nurse Clinician in Developmental Pediatrics, she works directly with families of children with autism spectrum disorders. Her graduate degree in educational psychology furthered her capacity to support children with special needs and to bridge the gaps between the medical world of developmental pediatrics and the educational world of the classroom. The revision of this book is an extension of her commitment to support children and families by offering current and relevant information. She continues to learn daily and in doing so, continues to be driven to share that growth and knowledge.

Anthony F. Malone is a pediatrician with a specialty in child development. In over 30 years of practice, he has worked with many families of children with a wide variety of developmental difficulties. In his role as Developmental Pediatrician he wears many hats. In addition to evaluating children and making recommendations to families, he also has the responsibility of educating up- and- coming pediatricians and other professionals in the field.

In addition to his time spent at the developmental pediatric office, Dr. Malone provides pediatric care to typical and special needs children in his active private practice. Dr Malone has much "hands on" parenting experience and genuine appreciation for the challenges of parenting, as well as the joys..

Index